D0389504

IDIOTS

ALSO BY LAURA CLERY

Idiot

IDIOTS

MARRIAGE, MOTHERHOOD, MILK & MISTAKES

LAURA CLERY

G

GALLERY BOOKS

NEW YORK   LONDON   TORONTO   SYDNEY   NEW DELHI

G

Gallery Books
An Imprint of Simon & Schuster, Inc.
1230 Avenue of the Americas
New York, NY 10020

Copyright © 2022 by Idiots, Inc.

Note to readers: Certain names have been changed whether or not so noted in the text.

All rights reserved, including the right to reproduce this book or portions thereof in any form whatsoever. For information, address Gallery Books Subsidiary Rights Department, 1230 Avenue of the Americas, New York, NY 10020.

First Gallery Books hardcover edition April 2022

GALLERY BOOKS and colophon are registered trademarks of Simon & Schuster, Inc.

For information about special discounts for bulk purchases, please contact Simon & Schuster Special Sales at 1-866-506-1949 or business@simonandschuster.com.

The Simon & Schuster Speakers Bureau can bring authors to your live event. For more information or to book an event, contact the Simon & Schuster Speakers Bureau at 1-866-248-3049 or visit our website at www.simonspeakers.com.

Interior design by Alexis Minieri

Manufactured in the United States of America

10 9 8 7 6 5 4 3 2 1

Library of Congress Cataloging-in-Publication Data has been applied for.

ISBN 978-1-9821-6710-3
ISBN 978-1-9821-6712-7 (ebook)

To my whisker biscuit, for pushing out the two most utterly perfect humans I know.

CONTENTS

Introduction

IDIOTS WELCOME!

So here we are, two kids later. HOW THE HELL DID THAT HAPPEN??!!

Sex. Sex is how that happened. To set the scene for you . . . no, not *that* scene . . . the scene from which I'm communicating with you. I'm writing this introduction while listening to a very avant-garde soundtrack: the shrill screaming of a toddler. Hold on real quick, I'm gonna go tell him to shut the fuck up, but I will translate it to: "Hey, sweetheart, it's okay to have big feelings, but Mommy is working in the next room so if you could just—aw, you want to play with purple sand? Ok then, I can just finish my work later." Stay tuned for more janky parenting tips!

You may be wondering, *Why is Laura writing her second book at the same exact time she had a second baby, is in the midst of postpartum depression, and when her toddler just got diagnosed with autism?* Good fucking question!

I've already told you the exciting stories from my drug-fueled life in my first book. Now all I do is breastfeed little aliens and go to bed at 9:30 p.m. I also drink an ungodly amount of coffee, and go on LOTS of walks. Riveting, I know. Maybe you're excited to find out what type of mother I am? So am I! You want birth stories? Fine, admittedly those are juicy—literally! How about my marriage? Want to know more about that? Because it's not the perfect #relationship goals union that you people seem to think it is. What marriage is? Seriously, if Jay-Z can cheat on Beyoncé, we're all fucked.

—

Early one morning, soon after my daughter was born, I was attempting to part ways with my postpartum depression by switching up the route on my daily serenity stroll. New route, new thoughts, new me? I don't fucking know. I was desperate. Oh, I should also mention that on this very personal, soul-searching stroll, I was accompanied by 14,000 strangers on the internet. I was hosting a Facebook Live, chatting to a small town's worth of strangers about how I still had to wear diapers because of the placental tissue that was continuing to exit my body. Just then, I spotted an ancient, ethereal vision of a woman walking purposefully up the steep suburban hill and brandishing a shimmering cane. She wore what looked like a powder-blue cotton kimono and an oversized pink sun hat, which she had perched upon her perfectly silver braids.

Since I have zero impulse control and infinite conviction, I HAD to meet this mystical goddess. I sprinted across the street to kindly accost her by introducing myself and my entourage of 14,000 strangers. We chatted a bit and it turned out she was a huge racist!

KIDDING. She was *just* as celestial and magical as I knew she would be. We soon learned her name was Anne and she was ninety-eight years old. She was once in the Navy, then was a cop in Detroit in the 1950s, then she worked for more than fifty years as an anesthesiologist, not retiring until the sensible age of eighty-two. She told me she walked those steep hills every day, even when she didn't feel like it. I was blown away, as were my 14,000 besties. I knew I had to ask her what her secret was before she . . . well . . . before she was carried to heaven in a whirlwind.

"So what's your secret?" I asked, and 14,001 souls anxiously awaited her answer. She arrayed her thoughts, looked at my phone camera with an assuring smile, and said, "Fitness, always . . . and the Mediterranean diet."

And just like that, she changed my life. I have been eating nothing but hummus and grape leaves for the past three months straight and it has been a gas (and a little gassy).

She went on to tell me what she believed to be her most important piece of life advice, as well as so many other truly treasured insights. I often wonder, *If I hadn't been willing to change my route that morning in a desperate attempt to crawl out of my anguish, would I have ever met her?* Thank goodness I did because there she was—my guru, my guiding light. My boss-ass, bad-ass, mystical-ass bitch: Anne. Obviously, I have now made that route my new daily path, and I have been blessed to see (and kindly accost) her at least thirty more times. Each time I consider it a miracle. She is a reminder to never relent, to keep trudging up that hill, even when my monkey-mind tells me to hide under the covers. I make sure to ask Anne the tough questions: What is the secret to lasting love? What is your biggest regret? Are Kegels worth the trouble? Happily, she has answered all of these questions, and I'll share her wisdom with you throughout this book.

INTRODUCTION

This isn't a how-to book because I don't know how-to. I cannot bake and I genuinely don't know what day it is (yes, I am still sober). I don't even know how to find my iPhone half the time, let alone provide the answers to life's toughest questions. The purpose of these stories is to tell you my painfully honest and sometimes hilarious perspectives as a woman, a mom, an artist, and a wife. Love it or put a pin in it for now, this is my truth. So hang on to your diaper, if that's where you're at—I've been there too. Though, right now tonight, I happen to be wearing coffee-stained sweatpants and a suspiciously moist nursing bra. And by comparison, that's practically date night, isn't it?

CHAPTER 1

Come Inside My Vagina

Childbirth is a miracle. It's a beautiful, sacred, personal experience that transforms you and gives you a purpose deeper than you've ever known. Which is exactly why I invited 26 million online strangers to watch me primally scream and aggressively push out my gooey baby. My first birth has over 62 million views on Facebook alone. So between that and my second birth, over 82 million people have seen my punani—and I don't even have an OnlyFans.

Maybe you're one of the lucky ones who has seen the videos of Alfie and Penelope's wildly different births? Or maybe you're frantically googling them right this second so you can watch. I'll wait . . . Or maybe you're recoiling in disgust as you imagine my mucus plug, placenta, and who knows what other bodily fluids gushing out in a gruesome (yet sacred) waterfall of actual human juice. If you're in the latter camp, we're just getting started, bestie.

I opened my last book by telling the story about that one time

I came out of *my* mom's vagina, so it's only natural that I now share the rich details of my babies' birth stories. It's time to shift the focus to *my* tunnel of love (and pain). For example, there's one heartfelt tale about the time that our son, Alfie, was yanked out of my body by a vacuum. It wasn't a Dyson Cyclone V10 exactly, but still. As terrifying as it was having a whole person forcibly sucked out of my body, it was also magical. The human and the vacuum. I'd rate that vacuum five stars on Amazon if I could: powerful suction, lightweight, and fits perfectly in narrow spaces like my pussy.

Next there was the time during Penelope's birth that I was on all fours in a hospital room shower, in agonizing pain, making primordial noises so guttural that Stephen thought I was dying. Because he couldn't live without me, he contemplated jumping out of the hospital room window. When he remembered that we had kids to take care of, he decided not to jump one story to his death. It's a sublime memory, really.

The second I got pregnant, I became weirdly obsessed with watching strangers give birth online. Birth vlogs, birth stories, basically anything to do with tiny humans barreling into the world through a birth canal. As a kid I loved writing and directing horror movies with my giant camcorder, so it makes perfect sense that as an adult I love to settle in with some popcorn and watch poorly shot homemade videos of hospital births, home births, epidural births, unmedicated births, water births, car births, I-didn't-know-I-was-pregnant births, and DIY births. Yes, you read that right: DO-IT-YOURSELF BIRTHS. No, seriously, that's a thing. Look up "freebirthing." It will blow your fucking mind. So yes, basically, if you've put your own birth video online, whether you were in a hospital or in a river, I have probably watched it several times. While eating snacks.

When I was pregnant with our son, Alfie, I forced Stephen to watch birthing videos with me. The snacks helped lure him in, but he was a reluctant viewer at first. Why he would not want to watch a bunch of strangers writhe around in agony, with blood and gunk flying around, is beyond me. Anyway, after watching Ricki Lake's *The Business of Being Born* I suddenly became skeptical of the military-industrial birth complex with its hospitals and C-section-happy doctors. The star of *Hairspray* had successfully convinced me to have a drug-free water birth . . . at home. Before watching that movie, I figured I would have a good old all-American hospital birth with a shit-ton of epidural on the side. This is what both my sisters and most of my friends did, after all. Besides, I was never known for having a high pain tolerance. I was the kid who was taken to the ER by my babysitter because I started hysterically crying about stomach pains and she didn't want me to die on her watch (which, at eight dollars per hour, was fair). My parents had to leave a New Year's Eve party, which I'm sure was *the* place to be in Downers Grove, Illinois, that night. They rushed me to the hospital, only to hear the doctor say that it wasn't terminal—I just had a stomachache because I had eaten too much rocky road ice cream. So, considering that rocky night of dairy-induced agony, an epidural seemed the sounder road.

Despite the fact that I apparently can't so much as eat ice cream without going to the emergency room, after watching Ricki Lake's movie, I decided to have a home water birth—with a doula, a midwife, and no pain meds. I had been inspired to make informed choices because the host of a trashy 1990s daytime talk show told me to. SHE WAS REALLY CONVINCING, you guys. As Tracy Turnblad said in *Hairspray*, "Things need to change, and I won't stop trying to change them." I'm not against hospital births, epidurals, and C-sections.

I truly believe that however you have the baby is a freaking miracle. During my first pregnancy, I just became set on having my baby in a no-drugs/home-birth situation. I didn't want to freebirth it, with no one around at all to help catch the baby or remind me that I'm just giving birth, not dying. I was convinced that this was the best path for me (and Stephen . . . but mainly me, for obvious reasons), so I bought a home-birthing tub and some evening primrose oil off the internet. It was all about to go down . . . my birth canal.

If you've seen the video of Alfie's birth, you probably know that things did not go according to plan. At all. It was like someone (God?) took my plan, crumpled it up in a ball, set it on fire, and then ran over the smoldering ashes with an eighteen-wheeler.

But before all that happened, about six months into my first pregnancy, I started looking for a midwife to help with the home birth. After careful, painstaking research, I finally found a woman I liked. I'll call her Maude. I stopped going to my regular OB-GYN except for the important 3D scans, which Maude couldn't do because she wasn't a doctor and her tool kit didn't involve electricity or any science whatsoever. That didn't bother me, though. She had good Yelp reviews!

Meeting Maude was like meeting the fairy godmother who would help bring my baby into the world in a relaxing, drug-free, miraculous way. I put all of my trust in her. Every time I saw Maude the Midwife, I felt that she was truly listening to me. She seemed to care so much about me as a whole person, not just a hole-person. She asked about my diet, how my relationship with Stephen was going, my sleep schedule, my emotional state, my sun, moon, *and* rising signs, my most embarrassing middle-school moment, my favorite brand of cereal, AND how my cervix was doing. It was such a nice change from the rushed feeling of going to the doctor's office and having cold gel squirted onto my stomach. At the doctor's office there was no "So how are you *really* doing?" But here was Maude, asking where I got my shoes and about the consistency of my discharge. I was into it!

The thing is, sometimes I can get excited about the Maudes of the world and overlook the red flags. I basically spent my entire teens and twenties doing this. Like the time I decided that because a strange guy I met ONCE wrote his name and number on a cocktail napkin and told me I should be a model, that was reason enough to get on a plane to New York City and MOVE IN WITH HIM. That decision worked out great, if you think falling for a dangerously abusive sociopathic drug dealer sounds great. Anyway, Maude's office was in Los Angeles and it was decorated in a modern hippie style with tie-dyed fabrics and crystals everywhere. The only thing missing was a lava lamp. Oh, and ANY MODERN MEDICAL EQUIPMENT AT ALL. I remember one day after an appointment, Stephen was freaking out because all of Maude's "medical equipment" looked like she'd borrowed it from the *Game of Thrones* prop room. It was all ancient torture device–type scales and prods that I hadn't really noticed before, maybe because I was so charmed by being asked about my relationship with my grandmother, how much gluten I consumed, and whether I believed in any conspiracy theories. She also asked what my primary emotional state was, but as a pregnant person, I couldn't pick just one! Irritable, terrified, anxious, thrilled, bloated, blissful, achy, horny, tired, hungry, nauseous, irate, itchy, stretchy, annoyed, and did I say tired? Is bloated an emotion? It should be! Maude listened to it all, without judgment. Or medical equipment. She was awesome.

Or so I thought.

"Laura, I don't know about this whole home-birth idea," Stephen said after one of our appointments with Maude. "Everything in her office is so . . . medieval. What if something goes wrong? How will we live with ourselves? And what is that iron thumbscrew-looking thing she keeps poking you with?"

"Stephen, it's FINE," I said. I was still very certain that the birthing tub I bought was a solid purchase, even though, in reality, when you're using a birthing tub the nice clear water soon looks like a vat of tomato-beef stew. I know this because I've watched precisely 679 water births online.

At my final, thirty-week, let's-squirt-gunk-on-your-stomach-and-look-at-your-3D-fetus scan with the OB-GYN, they told me that Alfie was measuring big, to which I replied, "Are you fat-shaming my fetus?" "No, I'm strongly suggesting that you and your big fetus ditch the tub and give birth at the hospital, just in case there are complications." When I later told Maude what they'd said, she confidently pulled out her cast-iron calipers from 1492 and measured my supposedly thick baby from the outside using the magical power of dowsing.

"Nope, this baby is the perfect size," Maude said, totally self-assured. "3D scans aren't always accurate," she said, dismissively waving her fireplace tongs. She was totally persuasive, whispering soothing anecdotal evidence and assuring us that our baby was "the perfect size." Then she lightly struck her massive gong, told us we had nothing to worry about, and we went on our way.

After the appointment I was like, "Okay, great, the baby is perfect!" And Stephen was like, "Bloody hell!"

A few weeks later, Stephen turned to me AGAIN, very nervous, and said, "Laura, I don't know about this home-birth idea. If something bad happened, how would we ever forgive ourselves?"

Still feeling totally confident about my birth plan, I assured Stephen that women have been giving birth at home for centuries (why did he think Maude's devices were so old?), and that natural home births are very popular in his home country, the U.K. Plus, about 1.6 percent of U.S. births happen outside of the hospital, which is huge! When Stephen still wasn't convinced by my stats, I decided to pull up Yelp reviews of Maude again. I would prove to him once and for all that we were in the best prenatal care, even if there was a didgeridoo stashed in the corner of her office. I had read her reviews before, of course, but a few months had passed since I'd looked. How much could change?

"Here, I'll show you, there is *nothing* to worry about!" I said as I pulled up Maude's Yelp page. It all seemed positive, but then I scrolled down further. My confidence in Maude instantly collapsed. I landed on a one-star review that shook me to the core.

"Laura, what does it say?" Stephen pleaded. Maybe he was tipped off by the fact that all the blood had drained from my face, or that I was sitting so silent and still it was as if my soul had temporarily evaporated, which it might have.

"One second," I said, skimming for other, better reviews.

"Laura!"

"Okay, fine," I said. I realized that I had to read this terrifying review to Stephen. I had to admit that he had been right about Maude and her torture gadgets all along. The review was written by a husband, and I'm paraphrasing, *but not by much*:

We had an extremely bad experience with Maude. There were red flags that were ignored, and my child almost died.

"Should I keep going?" I asked. Of course, Stephen said yes. How could we not continue down this horrifying path?

My wife had expressed concerns to Maude about the size of our son (he was over 11lbs. at birth) and she assured us there was no issue. We were so wrong to trust her. Home birthing an 11lb. child is never easy, and my son had the cord caught around his neck. When he was born he was not breathing and Maude couldn't revive him with CPR. We called 9-1-1, and I traveled with him to the hospital leaving my wife behind, bleeding and in shock. While they did manage to revive him in the ambulance, he had suffered brain damage and was in a coma for days. (He is alive now thanks to the incredible people at the hospital.)

Maude's manual assessment of our son's weight was inaccurate and irresponsible. If we had known his weight before the delivery we would have decided to deliver at the hospital birthing center. We have learned a valuable lesson: never let any "expert" have more power than your intuition. If you feel something is wrong, don't let anyone dismiss your concerns. Make sure you are confident that you have the answers!

My stomach felt sick, and Stephen looked like he was about to throw up. It seemed that this traumatized husband was telling OUR EXACT STORY. We had been told that Alfie was measuring big but were just hearing reassurance from Maude. It was the most disturbing thing Stephen and I had ever read, like we'd been trusting Jeffrey Dahmer to babysit. We were shaking. The father on Yelp also said he'd had to repost his review because it had been deleted. I guess that's why I missed it when I was investigating Maude initially. So long story long, I ended up returning that home-birthing tub the next day. And I returned Maude too.

As freaked out as I was, I'm not big on confrontation. I just emailed Maude, telling her it was best if we parted ways because our OB-GYN wants us to have a hospital birth. Here's the email (notice how I used the word "revert"—maybe to make her feel better?):

We wanted to let you know that we won't be coming in tomorrow afternoon because after much consideration, we have decided to take a different route with this pregnancy and are going to revert to using our OB-GYN.

We have been advised by our doctor that it would be safer to have a hospital birth this time around. We really wanted a home birth but we wouldn't be able to live with ourselves if something went wrong and we didn't take into account the doctor's opinion on his size and therefore the extra risk.

Thank you so much for all your help thus far. We learned a lot from you and so appreciated your time and care. Hopefully next time we can make it work.

Sincerely,
Laura and Stephen. ♥

PS. I downloaded Turbo Tax like you suggested, and also thanks again for the gluten-free vegan mac and cheese recipe.

Please note my addition of "*Hopefully next time we can make it work*" plus the heart emoji. Sometimes I make myself sick. I had

ZERO intention of EVER letting Maude near my gullible but well-meaning uterus ever again, but my people-pleasing character defect (PPCD) has not completely lifted yet. I'm still working on that one. Sorry, but I can't help trying to make people happy. Why am I apologizing? Why is it so hard to stop apologizing?! Even with my PPCD, why I cared about hurting HER feelings is truly a mystery. Okay, according to some random article on the internet, people-pleasing behavior comes from having poor personal boundaries and a longtime need for validation. Supposedly this behavior is more common in people with a traumatic family history or a history of toxic or abusive relationships. Okay yeah, all that checks out. Oh, it's also much more prevalent in women. Sorry that I got sidetracked, but I am NOT sorry for being a woman who has endured trauma. I mean, I AM sorry, but not *sorry* sorry. Sorry!

ANYWAY. Back to Maude. How did she reply, you might ask? Was she heartbroken, pleading with us to trust her with our precious, perfect child that she would deliver in the tub effortlessly, with her crude prods and scales? Did she want to sit and talk it out over a cup of red raspberry leaf tea? Meditate and bang a gong about it? Nope. This is what she replied:

> *Ok, sending all my best!*
> *Maude* ❀

That's fucking it! We'd been through so much together. She'd asked about my marriage, my vagina, my childhood obsession with infomercials and my most recent bank overdrafts. She told me she'd take care of us all, but she was happy to end it with a fucking rose emoji? Is it because roses oddly resemble vaginas and there's no bearded clam emoji (yet)? Probably.

At least her email didn't make me feel worse about the fact that we'd fired her. If Stephen hadn't had his doubts, and if I hadn't pulled up her latest Yelp reviews, we might have ended up in a horrible situation like that poor family.

I guess the point is that the universe works in mysterious ways, and you should always *double-check* Yelp reviews. Triple-check them. Check them once a day if a baby is involved.

After that horrible day, it was back to the OB-GYN for us. I still wanted an unmedicated birth, and not because I was scared of needles. I'm an ex–drug addict, remember? I wanted an unmedicated birth for other reasons:

1. My hero/incredible mom had all three of her daughters without pain meds.
2. I heard having an unmedicated birth makes for an easier recovery.
3. I wanted to prove to myself that I was stronger than I thought.
4. Ricki Lake told me to.

Like I've said, I have zero judgment when it comes to how any woman chooses to give birth. It's your vagina, so do what you want—just not with Maude!

At thirty-seven and a half weeks with Alfie, I started feeling Braxton Hicks contractions, which, if you're not familiar with them, are basically false/early labor pains. But that doesn't mean they don't fucking hurt. I'd heard that walking helps induce labor, so I forced Stephen to walk with me down the hill from our house. I'd also heard spicy food helps, so we waddled down to a Mexican restaurant so I could ingest a bowl of jalapeños. I was in the middle of guzzling hot sauce when a strong contraction came on, and right as I was mid-groan, some guy walked up to us saying, "Hey, I loved your video about road rage!"

So, being the consummate professional/people-pleaser that I am, I growled back, "THANK YOU SO MUUUUUUAAACH!" This probably made him think I was raging all the time and not just on the road.

Once the guy and my contraction went away, we finished eating. Just as we were ready to leave, two more jalapeño-induced contractions came on fast, and stronger than before. Stephen and I looked at each other romantically, like, "HOLY SHIT, IS THIS IT!?" We didn't even need to speak, we just *knew* exactly what the other person was thinking by the panicked looks in our eyes. We called an Uber, and our driver sped back to the house, terrified I'd unload my amniotic fluid in his Subaru. Everything stayed intact, and we got home ready to DO THIS. But wouldn't you know it . . . the contractions stopped. Maybe I should have eaten a habanero pepper instead?

What do you do at a time like that? A time when you think THE BIG MOMENT is happening, but then it stops, but then you know it could start again ANY SECOND? You watch *Romy and Michele's High School Reunion* for the twentieth time, quoting every line from memory, and then go to sleep, which is exactly what we did. (For the record, I'm the Mary and Stephen is the Rhoda.)

Later that night, I woke up to a giant gush of warm water. I knew it was my water breaking and not pee, because I peed myself daily in the third trimester, so I was a pro at knowing. I woke Stephen up. "BABE!! MY WATER BROKE! OH MY GOD! MY WATERBAG HAS BROKEN!!"

"Your *waterbag*?" he repeated, very groggy and possibly still dreaming of inventing Post-its. "That's a funny word, waterbag . . ." Then it hit him: "Oh my God! Oh my God!" he yelled with pure excitement/terror. "I've got to make some coffee!"

What. The. Fuck?

But then again, I wanted to labor at home for as long as possible, and I figured Stephen should be wide awake for the whole thing, so coffee wasn't the worst idea. And I did labor at home, until it was time to drive to the hospital. We followed the "5-1-1 rule," which is: Contractions are five minutes apart, lasting one minute long, for one hour straight. I feared if we waited longer than the 5-1-1 rule, we'd be calling 9-1-1. Once my contractions were coming faster than my high school boyfriend, we got into the car and headed to the hospital. When we walked into the check-in area, I was doubled over in pain. Instead of immediately asking, "How far apart are the contractions?" like they do in the movies, the guy behind the desk goes, "Hey, I follow you on Instagram!" I ONCE AGAIN growled, mid-contraction, "That's AHHHHHHHHwesome!" Then we took a photo. Ever a pleaser.

So back to that idea of childbirth being magical. I spent five hours in excruciating pain, unable to talk or breathe, sitting on a birthing ball making primitive noises, while a well-intentioned/ annoying nurse with an oversupply of empathy (yes, it's a thing) kept popping in to say:

"Do you want the epidural? If you get the epidural you won't feel a thing . . ."

To which I grunted, "No, I'm good."

Then, an hour later, she would come back:

"Do you want the epidural? If you get the epidural you won't feel a thing . . ."

"No thanks."

Then, later:

"Do you want the epidural? If you get the epidural you won't feel a thing . . ." Then, her eyes got wide and filled with secondhand pain: *"TRUST ME, IT'S ONLY GOING TO GET WORSE. I tried it with my first baby and it nearly killed me. DON'T DO THIS TO YOURSELF."*

To which I replied, "FUCK IT! GIVE ME THE EPIDURAL!"

At the end of the day, any way you have your baby is beautiful, and believe me, when I had that epidural, things got a lot more beautiful. I went from medieval torture levels of pain to forgetting I had legs. We laughed. I relaxed. My doula was in the room, but I haven't mentioned her so far because she was on her phone the whole time. She did take a break from scrolling Facebook every once in a while to put her hand on my back and say, "It's okay." In her defense, there wasn't much for her to do after I had gotten the epidural. I was just lying there numb, in zero pain, telling dick jokes to Stephen. I told her she could leave about three separate times. Truthfully, it was a little awkward having her just sitting there in the corner texting friends and playing *Candy Crush*, but she insisted on staying.

Then, after sixteen long hours, they told me I was fully dilated. If you know nothing about childbirth, "fully dilated" doesn't mean a giant trapdoor opens in your vagina and a baby pops out with no problems and plenty of elbow room. It means your cervix is now paper thin and has opened to ten centimeters wide, but you still have to PUSH A HUMAN THROUGH THE BIRTH CANAL. Apparently it was time for this magic to happen. Of course I had no clue it was time or what was happening inside my own body, because I WAS SO FUCKING NUMB. I loved the epidural, but I couldn't even feel the entire lower half of my body, let alone feel myself pushing. After I attempted to pushed for a while, I could tell that the nurses and doctors were feeling maybe a little bit frustrated. Then, their looks of frustration quickly turned to looks of real concern. I felt helpless, and I asked the doctor to turn the meds down. Still, I could feel nothing. My bulky baby's heart rate started dropping, so the NICU team came in, which is never a good thing. They put an oxygen mask on me, the doctor asked if I was okay with her using the vacuum, and I said, "Sure. Just DON'T use a cordless stick—the batteries are never reliable." What else was I supposed to say? I wanted to get Alfie out as safely and quickly as possible, with whichever household appliances got the best ratings on Amazon.

Stephen had an irrational, patriarchy-induced fear of watching the baby come out of my whisker biscuit, so when the doctor asked him whether he wanted to be on the business side (my head) or the party side (my pussy) when it was time, Stephen was all business. But when Alfie started crowning, Stephen immediately shoved the doula out of the way (not that she noticed) and watched our son come into the world in absolute awe and elation. He saw the entire thing and cried joyous, blissful tears.

There was little Alfie. He was perfect beyond compare and on my tit within two minutes. It was the best moment of my life so far. The video of Alfie's birth that you may have seen online is about twelve minutes of a SIXTEEN-HOUR experience—but we picked the best, most exciting parts.

With our daughter's birth, we also had a plan. But again, the joke was on us.

Here's one reason I love social media: There is a tribe of mamas out there who have your back and will listen to your problems no matter how many bodily fluids or secretions are involved. At twenty-nine weeks along with my baby girl, we had a pregnancy scare. I thought I'd lost my mucus plug, which isn't supposed to happen until shortly before you go into labor, and twenty-nine weeks was way too early. I made a doctor's appointment and tortured Stephen the whole way there by saying "mucus plug" as much as possible (try it with your partner, especially if they're squeamish). To help ease my fears, I'd asked via social media if anyone had advice, and what I got back were tons of reassuring comments along the lines of, "Girl, let me tell you about my mucus plug . . ."

Your disgusting stories were so heartfelt and graphic, I cherished every one.

The doctor did an ultrasound to check on the baby using modern medical devices instead of ancient divining rods (by this point Maude was a distant, but haunting, memory). She assured us that everything looked fine, and that my mucus plug was still intact!

"Are you sure?" I asked. This must be every physician's favorite question. They go through years of training and analyze ultrasounds all day long just so someone like me can ask, "But *how* do you know?

Because I posted a picture of it on Facebook and like four different strangers said it DEF was my plug . . ."

Anyway, she was 100 percent sure. So what the hell had oozed out of me? I guess all kinds of things can ooze out when you're pregnant and full of hormones. (I'm still convinced it was a tiny chunk of plug.) The baby was actually perfect (not Maude's tarot-card perfect, but medically perfect). Everything was fine, so we went back home to wait for the actual mucus plug to drop like an album, a book, or a movie that everyone is dying to see. Except it was a mucus plug, and no one on earth wanted to see it, not even me, except maybe I did a little. But Stephen absolutely did not.

When I was thirty-six weeks and five days along with Penelope, I started feeling a tightening in my stomach and I'd get slightly out of breath. I figured I was having false contractions again, because they didn't hurt and there was no way I was in labor this early. So what did I do? I turned to my online tribe of delirious mamas and I did a Facebook Live, asking the ladies what their early labor signs had been. As I was reading out comments of random women's early signs, every few minutes, I would continue to feel the tightening in my stomach . . .

"Kerry from Kansas says she was super horny when in early laaaaaaaabor—sorry, guys, I felt the tightening again. I'm sure it's just Braxton Hicks . . . right?"

Then, literally 100,000 women chimed in, saying things like: *"Labor and delivery nurse here—those are contractions!"*
Or:
"I'm 100 percent sure you're in labor. Go to the hospital immediately!"
I love you guys, but I didn't believe you yet. I was feeling zero pain, so I was sure this was not actual labor. What kind of wacko

does a Facebook Live while she is IN LABOR? Me! I do. I don't know what tipped people off to the fact that I was in labor, unless it was the fact that my Facebook Live went kind of like this:

"You guys, I don't think this is labor, it doesn't even huuuuuuuuuuuuuurt—that's tight."

Or . . .

"This can't be actual labor. I appreciate your comments but— *AHHHHHH WOAHHHHHH.*"

And then . . .

"I'm just going to stay home as long as—WHAAAAAAT WAS THAAAAAAT—maybe I AM in labor?"

You guys were right. I was in labor. On Facebook Live.

With Alfie, as soon as my water broke, I felt contractions so intense I couldn't even talk through them. On this day I felt the tightening, but I felt zero pain. Labor is supposed to HURT, and I was feeling no pain. There was something wrong. Where was the agony? Where were the cramps so excruciating you want to gouge out your eye?! (I would still like to be able to see with my other one.) That's what I was waiting for! Eye-gouging pain.

After the Facebook Live, I did call my doula to relay my symptoms, and she told me, "You're fine. Get a good night's rest, have lots of sex, take walks, and call me when things get crazy."

Okay . . .

Then, I called my OB-GYN, and she said, "You're fine. Have lots of sex, take walks, and come see me tomorrow so I can check you."

Also, okay . . .

After months of sleepless, sweaty, fifteen-pee-break pregnancy nights, I actually had the most amazing, deep sleep of my life that night. I slept consistently (no peeing), and I felt completely refreshed and relaxed the next day. When we saw the doctor, I imagined that she'd say I had been dramatic and that we had a few more weeks to go. Then she'd send me on my way to have lots of sex and take walks and call her with any changes.

But that's not what happened.

As I sat down on the table for the exam, I felt a trickle of liquid. It could have been urine, but since, remember, I was a highly qualified expert on peeing myself, I was pretty sure it was not piss. My OB-GYN did the exam, and she did not tell me to go have sex or take walks.

"Your water broke. And you're already three centimeters dilated and ninety percent effaced," she exclaimed. "You need to pack your bags and I'll meet you at the hospital."

"WHAT?! Wait. How broken is my water?" I asked, as if there were a sounding line to test whether it was rain-puddle broken or depths-of-the-ocean broken.

Then Stephen chimed in, "Hey, remember when you called it a 'waterbag'? Hahahaha!"

"SHUT IT DOWN, STEPHEN."

"Sorry."

The doctor looked irritated with us already.

"There's no way to quantify how broken your water is," the doctor said. "Your water either breaks or it doesn't."

I'm pretty sure she was ignoring a lot of nuance, but I'm no doctor. Obviously.

My cervix may have been ready to party, but I was feeling zero agony, and childbirth is all about agony, right? The only reason I'd even called my doctor at all was because of the 100,000 women on Facebook Live telling me to. My plan had been to labor at home as long as possible and then hop over to the maternity ward when I felt the urge to poo, no drugs involved. My dream was to make it *just* in time to not have a car baby. But here was my doctor telling me to forget the laboring at home, and not only that, she said she would probably need to induce me with Pitocin. Since my contractions were irregular and my water had broken, both the baby and I would be at risk for infection if I didn't have her within eighteen hours. It was such a blow, because I had heard that Pitocin was the devil's drug, meaning it made your contractions feel like a demon was writhing inside of you, a zombie was chomping at your uterus, like Mike Tyson was at war with your pelvic floor . . . I wanted to feel this birth in a natural way, and not in a Pitocin-y, thought-you-were-taking-a-hit-of-a-harmless-joint-but-it-turned-out-it-was-laced-with-bath-salts way.

"I've heard that some women have trickles for a week before they go to the hospital," I said, hoping that hearsay would convince my doctor that her years of medical school training and real-world experience had nothing on my Google searches.

"Well, a midwife would let you do that, and then I treat the babies and moms with infections because they labored at home too long." (THE SHADE.) She continued, "The goal is to not have a baby that winds up in the NICU, right?"

I found her comment to be a little manipulative and yet very convincing.

"Right!" I said.

"It's nice to plan things, but sometimes God has another plan," said the doctor. Did she not take into account that I could have been atheist, polytheist, or Kardashianist? How presumptuous of her to assume that I believe in an all-knowing Sky Daddy! Anyway, if she was trying to scare me into going to the hospital, it worked.

As soon as we left the OB-GYN office, I called the doula from the car.

"So apparently I'm three centimeters and ninety percent effaced," I told her.

"Fuck," she said in her most professional tone.

"Yeah," I said. "The doctor said we need to go to the hospital today and that she'll induce me, in case of infections."

"You don't need to go to the hospital."

Um . . . WHAT?

"I have echinacea and probiotics—you'll be fine!" said the doula. *What the fuck are those going to do*, I wondered. "You don't need to be induced, just let it happen naturally. Just because the doctor tells you to go in doesn't mean you have to," she said. "Take some castor oil."

I told the doula I'd heard not-so-great things about castor oil.

"You just diarrhea your brains out and then you diarrhea some more and your baby comes out," she said casually, trying to reassure me, I guess. "Your baby will just flow out in a river of shit. It'll be great."

Can we take a second and talk about the conflicting advice women get when it comes to childbirth, and labor, and our bodies, and raising kids, and being a mom, and breathing on this planet? But mainly about giving birth? Stephen and I were so confused by the polar opposite opinions. I did know one thing: I did not want to take castor oil because pushing a baby out in a river of shit sounded horrific. It all sounded horrific, to be honest.

"I need to think about it," I said, still shocked that I was in labor since I felt no pain.

"Look, go home, go for a long walk, don't have sex, and let it progress naturally," she said. "Whatever you decide to do, I support you."

The doula said this basically right after she called the doctor an idiot, but okay.

Then I called the doctor to ask her if I could labor at home for a while, and after she'd basically ordered me to the hospital an hour before, she said, "Sure that's totally fine, as long as you come to the hospital at some point today. Go on walks, but do not have sex or take a bath." So basically, she was telling me to come to the hospital filthy and horny. That was not a problem.

Finally, I'd gotten some advice that was at least sort of similar, even though my OB-GYN mercifully didn't recommend castor oil. So Stephen and I ate a big lunch, since my doula warned me that I wouldn't be able to eat anything once I was induced. We went on a long walk, and I kept feeling pressure, but no pain. Stephen had composed a whole soundtrack of soothing music for the birth, so we put that on, and since nipple stimulation is supposed to help with labor, Alfie cuddled into bed with me and breastfed. It was a magical time with the people I loved most. I had heard that second-time moms go faster when they deliver, so when my (not painful) contractions got closer together, I called my doula to see if we should head to the hospital.

"You don't need to go yet," she said. "Why don't I come over and we can go on a long walk and . . ."

"AHHHHHHHHH!!!" As she was talking, I had another contraction, and this one actually hurt. Then I had a second, more painful contraction. "AHHHHHHHHHHHH!!!!"

"Oh, never mind," the doula said. "Let's meet at the hospital."

We left Alfie with our amazing nanny Carla, and my mama was on her way to L.A. from Chicago to help. I'd spoken to her earlier in the day, when she informed me that her "goddamn flight was delayed." She was in the air by this point, but Stephen and I were off to the races.

We checked into the hospital around 5:30 p.m. Unlike when I had checked in for Alfie's birth, the person at the front desk did not recognize us or ask us for a selfie. Rude! Later on, a few of the nurses whom we'd never met would say things like "Hey, girl, how's Alfie?" or "How's the house renovation going? Did you decide on the light or dark oak?" Even though I'd posted online about choosing light or dark wood, it's sometimes startling to run into total strangers who know details about your home flooring. Yes, the nurses were peering at my *pelvic* floor, but somehow knowing about my wood choices felt way more personal. I just didn't anticipate talking about my caulking while being fingered in the cervix.

Like I said, I had a whole plan for how this birth would go down. It would happen quickly, since this wasn't my first rodeo. I would do it without medication and it would be Zen as fuck. When I checked in, I was four centimeters dilated and still feeling no pain. I was weirdly *enjoying* labor and without pain meds. The doula arrived and immediately dimmed the fluorescent lights, lit candles all over the room, and used several dozen essential oils to soothe me. She even gave me a massage, and it was the most chill shit you've ever seen. It really put the "spa" in hospital. This birth was going to be EASY.

It may have been a relaxing vibe, but it wasn't fast like I'd planned. I'd been on intermittent fetal monitoring, which meant I could move around freely every twenty minutes. Sometimes I'd walk the halls and play ding-dong-ditch by knocking on random doors and waddling away (until I got in trouble). As the hours went by, wandering around the labor room was getting old. At 10 p.m. they checked me and I was only at 4.5 centimeters. I remember thinking, *Am I an idiot for not getting the Pitocin?* At midnight I hadn't progressed at all. The nurses were basically like, "You're an idiot for not getting the Pitocin!" Not in so many words; they said it in their TONE.

I was then told that only the top part of the amniotic sac had ruptured, so there was more breaking to be done (I TOLD YOU THERE WAS NUANCE!). The nurses said they could either break my water to speed things up with an instrument that, to me, looked like my Aunt Denise's crochet needle on steroids, or I could start the Pitocin.

"Does breaking my water hurt?" I asked meekly.

With a kind smile, one of the nurses said, "YES!"

So the crochet needle was a hard no. I agreed to start a light dose of the Pitocin to speed things up. What I didn't realize was that they administer the Pitocin through an IV. I don't know why I had it in my head that it was like a flu shot or something. Instead I was enduring contractions with a painful IV in my wrist—connected to a large BAG of Pitocin that was connected to an entire wheeled table. The bag of devil juice wasn't duffel bag–sized, but it wasn't clutch-sized either. I felt chained to this stupid table and bag full of a drug that I knew was going to bring me PAIN. I kind of yearned for the crochet needle in my hoo-ha, which I had perhaps too haughtily rejected.

A few hours after the IV, my contractions were still manageable. I was still dilating very slowly, which was frustrating since the drug is supposed to *move things along.* If I was going to walk around uncomfortably attached to a coffee table with no coffee, I needed it to ACTUALLY FUCKING WORK. Here's the thing with Pitocin. It starts off innocently, like your love-bombing narcissistic ex-boyfriend, but then after you've spent some time together, it quickly and cruelly turns into THE DEVIL on a BAD DAY. By 6 a.m., it was becoming harder to talk. But I still felt like, unless I couldn't get a single syllable out of my mouth, I could have this baby without an epidural. I was getting plenty of syllables out: *AHHHH* and *UGHHHH* and *FUUUUUUU* were not a problem to say, at all. I tried some HypnoBirthing breathing techniques, and then the doula piped up and suggested we do some nipple stimulation.

"Okay, I'll take the left one," she called out, "Stephen, you take the right!" They were both twisting my nipples simultaneously when the nurse walked in.

"Oh, sorry! Am I interrupting something?" Did she think I'd thrown an impromptu orgy . . . in labor? That I'd worked out an ethical adult arrangement between myself, my doula, and my husband under the fluorescent hospital lights while hooked up to an IV?

"No," I demurred, "you're not interrupting."

My plan of having a snappy two-hour labor was long gone. I was pissed. If I'd stayed and labored at home I could have at least done this part in my bedroom, with my on-screen besties Romy and Michele. Then again, the doctor wanted to monitor me, so arguing with a professional, especially when it concerned my baby, seemed foolish. That's the thing—you can make a plan, but the universe might have another one. You can prep, visualize all you want, but sometimes an easy, two-hour delivery is not in the cards—no matter how many perineal massages you endure, how much primrose oil you shove up your cooter, or how much clary sage oil you aggressively snort out of the bottle.

They'd been upping my dose of devil juice over time, and things had been pretty smooth and tolerable.

Until they fucking weren't.

When the pain intensified (and by "intensified" I mean it was a 7,000 out of 10) the sounds coming out of my throat were so primal, I actually thought they were coming from *outside* my body. Like, were there wild hyenas or hippos loose in the hospital, because that *can't* be me, can it? It could be and was. I never knew I had these noises in me to make. It was actually kinda awesome, in an excruciating kind of way.

I was shaking and crying from the intense waves, and my contractions were getting closer together. It was NOT fun anymore. There was no more spa in hospital, the orgy was definitely a bust, and I just wanted the pain to stop. But my baby said, "Nope, Mama. We're only just getting started."

A few months earlier, my doula had suggested that we pick a "safe word" to indicate the difference between pain and actual suffering when I was in labor. When I felt like I was suffering, I was supposed to use this word to let them know that maybe I actually did need an epidural. So Stephen and I put a lot of serious thought into what this word would be. It couldn't just be "ouch" or "uncle." It needed some *je ne sais quoi*. I decided that it should be a word I'd be embarrassed to scream in front of the nurses, since then I'd be less likely to give in and get the epidural. So after much meditation and serious contemplation, I decided the safe word should be . . . BALLSACK.

"But you definitely *would* want to scream that word in front of the nurses," Stephen puzzled.

"You're right, I would," I conceded. Still, *ballsack* it would be. My doula was thrilled.

And then, after around ten hours of being physically and emotionally assaulted by Pitocin-induced contractions, I finally knew what she meant by "actual suffering." I happily caved:

"BALLSACK! BAAAAAALLLLLSAAAACK!!!!! BAAAAA AAAAALLLLLLLLLLSACK!!!!!!"

Because I was in my own world of pain—my own planet of agony and physical torture—I have no recollection of how the nurses or anyone else reacted. The hyenas and hippos, *c'est moi*.

"BALLSACK! Why does anyone give birth?! BALLSACK! Why do women go through this?! BALLSACK!! BALLSAAAAAAACK!!"

In between screaming BALLSACK and primal grunting, I was weeping. The pain was now excruciating and I wanted that fucking epidural. Or to be back at the ethical adult party with the essential oils and soft music and dual-induction nipple twisting. I kept secretly hoping that the overly empathetic nurse from my first birth would come to my rescue. She would glide in with her sweet sorrowful eyes asking me, did I want to stop the pain once and for all? But . . . she never came.

This time, I screamed loud enough to rattle the windows:

"DICK PILLOW-ASS CURTAIN-SCROTES!!! CHANGEPURSE-CHIN-SLAPPING GRANDMA-FUCKER!!! BALLLLLLLLSAAAAACKKKKKKKKKK!!!!!!!!!!!!!!!!!!!"

Stephen got the memo. He ran out to find the anesthesiologist faster than a swift antelope being chased by a famished cheetah. He was told that the anesthesiologist was assisting with a C-section and it would be TWO HOURS before I could get relief. When he returned with the bad news, looking like the defeated cheetah that did NOT catch the antelope, I braced myself for more suffering.

I writhed, moaned, titty-twisted myself, and screamed BALLSACK, with no end in sight.

My doctor walked in on me nearly convulsing on the bed, making noises like I was expelling an evil spirit from my body. (Check it out on YouTube, smash that "like" button!) She looked at me with equal parts pity and terror and said we could take out the Pitocin so I could at least convulse around freely. My IV was out and the table was detached. I was free to move, so the doula dragged me to the bathroom, telling me that warm shower water was like a natural epidural. And guess what?

IT FUCKING IS NOT!

It wasn't a natural epidural in any way, BUT it did help bring my pain from a 7,000 to a 6,999. I actually felt safe in that little dark bathroom shower, and I was able to relax a little. If by relax you mean nearly passed out, unable to respond to anyone no matter how much I tried, curled over on the hospital shower floor, in absolute anguish. Growing up, we had two Siamese cats named Katie and Michael, and we had absolutely no reason for naming them that. Anyway, Katie was always having kittens because Michael kept knocking her up, and whenever she went into cat labor she'd always go hide in a dark corner or under my parents' bed. She did this because it felt safe. What I'm saying is that in that moment, I TOTALLY UNDER-STOOD KATIE. I wasn't in a fluorescent-lit hospital room with strange nurses walking in and out—I was in a small dark shower with hot water beating on me. It felt natural. Primal. It felt safe. I had finally stopped fighting the pain, and made the decision to let go and surrender to the pain and just accept exactly where I was at. Then, what do you know, it became *slightly* more manageable. I surrendered to the moment in that dark steamy shower, consciously relaxing my body and just letting it work for me. And then suddenly, I felt an intense urge to push. I started moaning, less of a scream . . . more a deep guttural groan. I would actually say this was my favorite moment. It was the most intense feeling in the world. Stephen popped his head in as I was mid-moan.

"Laura? Are you alright?"

I wasn't capable of using language at that moment. My contractions were longer and stronger and I had gone totally inward. The rest of the world didn't exist. It was getting really hot and steamy in there and I became nauseated, so I pushed the shower door open to let in some fresh air, which unfortunately let a shit-ton of water out. Water overflowed and FLOODED into the hospital room. The nurses came slipping and sliding in, because seriously, the hospital room was COVERED with water. It was absolute chaos. They frantically started drying the floors with towels, and by my specific deep groans it became very obvious that I was now in transition. I was in full squatting position and my body began pushing without me. I couldn't control it. I was grunting, moaning, and wailing with this undeniable urge to push. My sweet baby was finally ready to meet us and she was making it VERY clear. The nurses and doula took notice and hurried for the doctor. Within minutes, my doctor came sliding in across the flooded floor and nearly broke her damn neck.

"We are NOT about to have this baby on the bathroom floor!" my doctor yelled. "GET HER ON THE BED NOW!!"

So it turns out when I started screaming BALLSACK I was transitioning to the push phase, which explains the intense pain I was experiencing. From the countless birth stories I had watched on YouTube, it was ALWAYS the same thing: the very moment the women think they can't do it anymore, the moment they completely lose control and confidence in their ability to birth their baby, is right when their baby is ready to enter the world. I should have known I was so close. The nurses dragged me onto the delivery table. I was still naked, drenched, and on all fours, groaning, and the doctor said she could see the baby's head. But then, all of a sudden, I lost the urge to push. I tensed up because instead of being in the dark private shower, I was now in a bright room with a bunch of strangers looking at my privates. I had stage fright, or rather my butthole did, but the doctor said it was time to push.

"Push like you have to poo!" she said.

You know I'm a pleaser. I followed her directions and shat everywhere. I was briefly humiliated, but I was so in the flow-state the embarrassment went away and I just kept pooing. I was not in the headspace to distinguish between pushing a baby out and shitting. "Push like you have to poo!" she kept saying. I bet that after my delivery, the doctor changed up her instructions because I really went there. I was the valedictorian of shitting myself.

"Stop screaming! Push with your mouth closed!" she said. Why was the doctor so mad at me? Was it because I shat on her? Fair enough. All I wanted to do was moan it out, since it was very effective pain management for me, but she wanted me to use that screaming energy to push. So I shut my mouth, and then I pissed everywhere.

"You can do this, Laura!" Stephen said, helping me remember how to breathe.

The doctor stuck her fingers in my vagina and said, "Push where you feel my fingers." Considering I had just pissed and shat everywhere, it was an extremely bold move on her part. It actually did help me understand how to push, so I started pushing, and groaning, and breathing through the pain. With Alfie, I'd had the epidural, so I didn't feel the pushing in this way, and I suddenly understood why they called the feeling of the baby crowning and then finally emerging the "ring of fire." It really was a ring—of fucking fire! And there is no way to put it out! I strangely didn't mind the sensation, though, because I just wanted it over with, and the fire meant we were close to done. It hurt so good.

I could feel her head emerging, and then before we knew it, in two more pushes, there she was. The nurses gave her to me immediately, as we let the umbilical cord blood drain. I wish I could say it was a magical moment and I fell instantly in love. But it wasn't and I didn't. I was too shaken from the pain. I could barely hold her, let alone enjoy the moment. It was so wildly different from Alfie's birth. When they put Alfie on my chest, I had that feeling of pure blissful bonding that you hear about and see in movies, but with my baby girl, it didn't happen right away. I was so shaken up from hours of torment, and I just could not stop shivering and whimpering no matter how hard I tried. I cried and had an ever-so-quick moment of joy when I locked eyes with my beautiful Penelope, but it gave way to physical shock. I remember thinking that it was too intense and wondering why anyone ever does this without drugs. I felt so completely out of control and wondered when the shaking would finally stop. WOULD IT STOP?! I just wanted to marvel at my baby, but I could not. I kept letting out these involuntary, high-pitched moans that sounded like a dying bird. It was not picture-perfect, at all. I asked Stephen to take off his shirt and cuddle our baby, so I could (hopefully) calm down.

I remember feeling enraged. I was infuriated that it wasn't the euphoric moment I had been promised, or that I'd hoped for. The high wasn't there, just the pain. I was so angry in that moment that

I had done this to myself, glaring at the doula and silently scream-ing, *You fucking liar, you're the reason I didn't get the epidural! You promised me a blissful birth. You lied to me. There is nothing blissful about this moment, I'm fucking covered in my own shit and piss, and I can't stop shaking and moaning, let alone hold my baby.* I kept that to myself, though. Classic pleaser.

For the first hour after Alfie's birth, I felt fantastic. It was the most magical time ever; then, about an hour later, I felt like I'd been run over by a freight train once the drugs wore off. This time, without the epidural, was another experience entirely. It was the exact opposite.

Turns out I just needed a little time to come back into this reality—my body needed time. Before the birth, I weirdly had been more scared of delivering the placenta than my actual baby. In one of the 25,000 birth vlogs I'd seen, a woman wasn't able to push her placenta out and so the doctor just shoved her hand inside and yanked it out. I think that story scarred me permanently. The mom said it was the worst pain of her life. I think I told my doctor like thirty times that I wanted to deliver my placenta naturally and to not put her hands inside me. I was also terrified of being stitched up without pain meds. That thought literally kept me up on multiple nights, but when it came time to actually do it, I was fine. I told her to use a lot of numbing Novocain and BOOM, it was done. NO BIGGIE!!! Why did I spend all that time during pregnancy worry-ing about those two things that ended up being NO BIG DEAL? I got through it, and all that worry was a waste of precious time. My whole philosophy is to focus on what I DO want rather than what I DON'T want, but sometimes that's easier said than done. (It's least easy when someone is stitching up your freshly torn front-butt while you're lying there covered in your own piss, shit, and blood, in full view of seven strangers.)

The nurses graciously cleaned me up. They iced my vagina, gave me Motrin, and within about an hour I felt like I was on top of the fucking world. Higher than a star above the North Pole. I came back to earth and *finally* felt that indescribable high that I had heard so much about. *Oh, this is what Miss Doula was talking about.* Ahh yes . . . THIS was bliss. This was nirvana. PURE elation, blessedness, ecstasy, transported to a perfect dreamworld where NOTHING negative could touch me. If Cloud Nine is the happiest cloud, I was on Cloud Ninety. It was better than any drug I'd ever consumed, and I am not an unknown in that field. My vibrations were soaring. I finally fell intensely and utterly devoted and in LOVE with my beautiful, perfect eight-pound, one-ounce, twenty-one-inch miracle, Penelope. I couldn't stop crying about how perfect and amazing she was, and I felt such a bond and a connection with her. Within thirty minutes I went from "Fuck you, doula, I will never do this EVER again—even if my life depended on it I would rather simply PASS AWAY!!" to "Stephen, we are definitely having an all-natural home water birth next." I was ready to have triplets in a forest with no Pitocin or Motrin in sight. I was planning to give birth on a rocky cliff by the ocean BY MYSELF. I was gearing up to shit and piss myself and moan and pray to the god of Ballsacks many more times in life, all in the name of motherhood!

After Alfie was born I was getting heavy pain medication, since the postpartum after the epidural was so terrible. This time when the nurses asked if I needed any medication, I was like, "No, I'm good." Truthfully, I felt fucking amazing! Even with a second-degree tear!

Stephen and I ordered vegan burgers and fries and stuffed our faces, and we laughed (and cried) about what we'd just been through. At what I'd just been through.

I'm still not sure whether my recovery was SO night and day between baby one and baby two because it was my second rodeo and the way of my pussy had been paved, or because I didn't have the epidural, so the aftermath wasn't such a horrible shock because I had already been through the worst of it. In the end, there's no real way to avoid the inevitable pain of childbirth—it's either going to happen mostly during labor if unmedicated or after . . . or both. But in my humble opinion, it is TOTALLY and UTTERLY worth every moment of agony. Every. Fucking. Moment.

Throughout most of my life, people looked at me as someone who had a low tolerance for pain (I recently went to urgent care for a cold). When I was pregnant, I always doubted I was strong enough to deliver a baby without pain medication. My sisters actually laughed when I told them I wanted to go all natural with Alfie, since they had so many memories of me having meltdowns over stubbed toes and flecks of dirt in my eye as a kid. But I wanted to see if I was strong enough, and I was. Perhaps in part because the anesthesiologist was busy and unavailable. SO I DID IT. I literally had no other option. I do like to think I gave the nurses a good story to tell their families and friends, screaming BALLSACK over and over at the top of my lungs with no conceivable explanation. For hours after Penelope's birth, Stephen looked at me like I was a goddess, a warrior queen. Had he completely forgotten that I pooped all over the nurses and doctor and maybe on him? But I had done it! The anesthesiologist was busy and so I DID IT! It was a totally unreal, utterly blissful time for us. Then, as we were immersed in this peaceful dreamworld . . . there was a loud-ass knock on the door.

"Come in," we said, expecting a nurse. Instead, a big, burly security guard stepped in, looking mad as hell. He stared straight at Stephen and commanded, "I need to talk to you, outside."

Then the security guard saw me, and then he looked back at Stephen, then back at me, and his furious expression quickly changed. "Aw, man," he said in a defeated tone. "This is gonna suck."

Stephen and I were so confused, until this once-scary security guard said, "I love your videos, and my wife, Lisa, loved your book. We're such big fans, guys." The once-intimidating guard became bashful. "Oh man . . . this is really gonna suck, but the nurses told me to ask you guys to stop filming in the halls. Like, I don't care that you film . . . it doesn't bother me at all . . . but they told me to tell you to stop . . . If it was up to me I'd say let's shoot a fuckin' movie right here right now, but you know, they're not cool with it or whatever, so . . . I'm so sorry about that. Anyway, have a great stay, you guys are awesome!"

And with that he left.

Looking back, I feel so grateful that the anesthesiologist was tied up with a C-section when I desperately cried out "ballsack," my safe word echoing safely through the labor ward. Because if the anesthesiologist had been available, I would have 200 percent numbed the shit out of my lanky lower half without question. I would have also missed my goal to go unmedicated. I almost gave up, but God or fate or just a really busy anesthesiologist intervened, and I'm forever grateful. This backbreaking birth . . . this laborious *labor* really did teach me that I am capable of overcoming anything. And that just when I think I can't go on . . .

It turns out I motherfucking can!

Provided there's no easy access to drugs on-site . . . sigh.

For me, it's similar to getting sober. When I was using and drinking, I was partially just numbing the pain of whatever was going on because it was too much (or so I thought) for me to feel. The less of my own face I can feel, the better. On my one-year anniversary of being sober, I got upset about something. Maybe a fight with Stephen, maybe writer's block; I really can't remember. That's how trivial it was. But I desperately wanted to numb out, so I contacted my dealer via Facebook, since I had deleted his cell number at the request of my terrifyingly inspirational sponsor. My ex-dealer told me to meet him at his house in ten minutes and he'd have my gram of mediocre blow ready for me. I drove over, totally anxious, and texted him that I was outside. He texted back that he was in traffic, and he'd be five minutes late. As I sat in my cluttered Mini Cooper, I remembered one of the tips my sponsor had drilled into me: "If you feel like using, call me first. You can still use, but just let me know before you do anything."

Right. Okay, I can do that. I mean, I'm definitely 100 percent going to get coked up off my tits. Nothing was going to stop me from numbing my own face . . . But . . . why not let her know first? Didn't make much sense to me, but I did it. Maybe it was the pleaser in me, but I called.

She didn't pick up.

THIS was a sign. I was meant to relapse on my one-year-sober birthday. I was meant to celebrate it by getting zooted.

"Two minutes away," my dealer texted . . .

My nerves kicked in. *I can't believe I'm here. I can't believe I'm doing this. I can't believe my obsession to use is so strong and in just 120 seconds I'm going to be hopped up on coke.* And just THEN my motivating little bitch-ass sponsor called back.

"Hey, you called?"

"Oh yeah, just wanted to give you a heads-up, I'm about to buy a gram of blow. Would be more, but shit's expensive out here in these North Hollywood streets. Okay, that's all, bye!"

"WAIT," she said with a weirdly calm urgency. "That's fine. Buy the drugs, but I know it's your one-year birthday and I'd love to give you a cake. There's a meeting at the West Hollywood log cabin and I just want you to celebrate. THEN you can go buy your drugs, but first, let me give you a cake. A year is a long time and a big deal."

I still wasn't convinced. And I sure didn't want a fucking cake. They're never even vegan. And truthfully, it's super creepy when a bunch of recovering crackheads you barely know sing a slow, sinister, off-key "Happy Birthday" and at the end of the song they somehow make it worse by adding "keep comingggg baaaaack . . ." Anyway, reluctantly, I agreed. The pleaser.

I met her at the log cabin meeting, took my non-vegan cake that I couldn't even eat, and sure enough, the obsession to use had lifted. All I had to do was call someone. Reach out. Get through that specific moment even though I never thought I could.

That was ten years ago, and I still haven't bought the coke I was promised. When I think of wanting to numb the pain of childbirth, and asking for the anesthesiologist, and having to wait, and how close I came to not achieving a goal, it reminds me of that one-year-sober birthday. Instead of my sponsor, this time it was a shower, and within minutes I had the urge to push. Was that God? Fate? The universe?

Whatever it was, Penelope Marilyn Hilton (Poppy for short) came into the world at 8:19 in the morning, at eight pounds, one ounce, and twenty-one inches long, and she was perfect. And I was strong enough to walk through my fear . . . even though to get there I had to shit and piss myself and scream BALLSACK at innocent people.

CHAPTER 2

Oh, the Places I've Pooped

First of all, a *TRI*mester cannot have four parts.

Yet someone (I see you, Dr. Harvey Karp) decided that the twelve weeks after childbirth needed to be part of pregnancy, and seen as a time when your baby is adjusting to not being in a cozy, undisturbed warm bath of a womb and pushed into this bright, obnoxious, noisy, sometimes too cold, sometimes too hot world that is outside its mother's insides. Also, you're adjusting to life with your baby (burping, breastfeeding, blowouts). It's a time of intense physical and emotional change when we not only are acclimating to our new bundle of joy but to life as a new mom. The concept makes no sense until you're in it, covered in spit-up that could belong to your baby *or* you. It's hard to say. You're both pretty much just hanging on by the cloth of your diapers, vulnerable, sleep-deprived, and caked in biological gunk. BUT THE CUDDLES ARE AWESOME.

When I was going into labor with Penelope, my doula was confident that "because it's your second, it'll just pop right out! Fast and easy-peasy!" She made second-time childbirth sound like the difference between sweating over a six-course home-cooked meal and ordering a delivery pizza. Birth number two would only take about forty-five minutes without traffic and arrive on my doorstep, warm, yummy, and covered in red sauce. Even my doctor assured me that second births are EASY. It was going to be like a party thrown just for me, a goddess who felt no pain and smelled like jasmine all day long. A vegan pizza–eating goddess whose birth would be so easy, she wouldn't even know the baby had arrived until someone interrupted her second slice to say, "Excuse me, so sorry, but a perfect baby just came out of your vagina and it was so quick and painless, you didn't even notice. Also, there's a bit of marinara on your leg you'll want to take care of."

That is exactly how it would be . . . *according to my doctor and doula.*

Well, they were so fucking wrong. Okay, I may have been a goddess, but I was the gross goddess who flung a butt burrito on my doctor's face and then smelled of spit-up, wee-wee, and soiled diapers for the next twelve weeks. Last I checked, Yankee Candle doesn't offer that scent combo. You know what, though? If Gwyneth Paltrow can make a "This Smells Like My Vagina" candle, I am definitely developing Pissy Raindrops, Sour Tit Milk, and Diaper Superbloom organic wax votives. Available soon at boibs.com.

The only person who was completely, brutally honest with me about childbirth and postpartum was my friend Jill, whom I've known forever. "Forever" meaning since elementary school. Like my other childhood friends Maggie, Jack, and Holly, Jill moved to Los Angeles from Illinois. They don't even work in entertainment, which is the usual reason why so many people come to L.A. They just wanted to escape the unforgiving cold of the Midwest and pay a lot more rent in exchange for not having icicles form on their faces all winter long. Anyway, we all ended up in the same city *and* we all happened to have kids pretty close together, but Jill was first. And she did not hold back when it came to telling us about every gruesome detail of her pregnancy and childbirth and postpartum experience. There were no promises of "it'll be great" or "you got this." And while I appreciated her honesty, she could have lied to my face like a decent human being.

Jill was my one rich friend growing up. She lived in a six-floor house one town over from us, and somehow, even though she had six floors to choose from while the rest of us had one or two, she was surprisingly not a dick. She was a nice, humble rich person, and she'd have us over for epic sleepovers. We would steal her parents' liquor, and they could never tell we'd taken it, because they were six floors away from us in a bunker under the farthest wing of the house.

Jill gave birth some months before me, Holly, or Maggie, so she was our resident expert. She told us horror stories about how tough postpartum was, scaring us all to death as we hung on her every word. She didn't mention anything about massage oil or being a jasmine-scented goddess. She was more like:

"Your perineum will tear and the stitches will feel like a tiny evil elf is stabbing your vagina for two to four weeks straight, minimum. Actually, I'm wrong. It'll feel like a thousand tiny evil elves with a dagger in each little hand."

"Get ready for raging hemorrhoids! SITTING DOWN will be a thing of the fucking past."

"You'll need stacks of oversized diapers to soak up the massive amounts

*of bleeding that'll pour out from your fur-burger every day for weeks . . .
Did I say POUR? Like a biblical flood."*

*"The wound inside your uterus is as big as the dinner plates at Cheese-
cake Factory."*

*"Did I mention engorged breasts? They're HORRIBLY PAINFUL . . .
They'll make you want to die, but you can't, because you have a baby to
feed and zero free will at all. None."*

*"Your brain will stop working, and you'll barely remember your
name. You won't remember your kid's name, the state you live in, or
your partner's name. No one will have names. It'll just be 'Hey you . . .'
or 'Kid . . .' or 'Hello, nameless baby . . .' or 'Person over there, whoever
the fuck you are, hand me the breast pump.' "*

". . . cracked nipples."

*"Showers? They will soon be a part of your past! A distant memory.
An illusion from a bygone era that fades with each passing day. And you
will smell like literal shit and not even care."*

*"My friend ripped and tore so much that her butthole joined forces
with her whisker biscuit and her buttussy (butt/pussy) is still bleeding a
month later, but there is nothing she can do but wait it out, in pain, while
keeping her baby alive. But life isn't about her or her butthole anymore,
it's about her child and her child's butthole . . ."*

I had *just* finished reading Ina May Gaskin's book of positive
birth stories. It seriously warned readers to consume only positive
childbirth stories—and then Jill stopped by. Fucking Jill and her
six-story house didn't get the memo. You're never supposed to scare
a first-time mom by talking about bleeding butts and torn anything.
Oh shit—I should have included a trigger warning at the beginning
of this book for first-time expecting moms who may be reading this.
It's not too late . . .

TRIGGER WARNING! TORN EVERYTHING!

So, after Jill scarred my mind and soul with postnatal nightmares, I decided to continue to read about and/or watch only positive birth stories so I could focus on what I *did* want (sparkly rainbows and orgasmic contractions) versus what I did not want (engorged anything, adult diapers, tearing from any and all holes, imaginary elves stabbing my front butt). Even though Jill painted a picture of postpartum life that robbed me of any and all sleep for three weeks straight, she is actually the nicest person I know. That's saying a lot because I'm from the Midwest, where literally everyone you meet is nicer than what you'd imagine Tom Hanks to be.

Jill is the friend who happily threw the most elaborate, detailed, over-the-top-baby showers for all of us. She spoiled us as kids and as adults. She's a lovable oddball whose lifelong *South Park* obsession causes her to link *everything* in life back to that show. "We went to this new restaurant and it was just like that Mexican restaurant where Cartman sabotages Kyle's birthday," or "Postpartum life reminds me of that one *South Park* episode where Kenny is killed because he sticks tampons up his ass, causing him to burst into a ball of blood!"

That's a real episode, by the way.

Jill eased up on the gruesome *South Park* comparisons when she had her second kid, because the birth and postpartum experience were much more positive for her. Jill said her second birth and recovery were a literal euphoric dream. Quick labor, easy recovery . . . I LOVED hearing that story. Jill and Maggie were both Team Epidural, because WHY pain? Whereas Holly and I, not so much. We were massaging each other's perineums with organic coconut oil while meditating to HypnoBirthing tracks. But as we've discussed, childbirth rarely, if ever, goes as planned, and Holly learned that the hard, excruciating, what-the-actual-fuck-is-happening-to-my-insides way.

Per her doctor's stern recommendation, Holly was induced at forty weeks and she was in labor for—OMINOUS DRUMROLL TO HEIGHTEN THE TENSION, PLEASE—FORTY-NINE HOURS!!! I wish this were an exaggeration. When she was over thirty hours in labor, with NO pain meds, no sleep, and hooked up to the HIGHEST dose of Pitocin available, she STILL insisted on working through it naturally, breathing through the intense pain to achieve the orgasmic birth we read about on hypnobirthinghub.com. I could NEVER have lasted that long. Just then, as she was starting to hallucinate and not in a good way, a nurse came in and told her that she was seven centimeters dilated and was SO close to meeting her baby. So Holly kept fighting through the intense waves, assuming she'd transition at any moment. Then, FIVE MORE HOURS went by in which the blinding pain continued to intensify and STILL NO BABY. Her doctor finally came in to check her again. And then, the unthinkable happened. The doctor looked up from between her convulsing, distressed legs, with a shock-stricken look on her face. "What?! What is it?!" Holly moaned. "I'm so sorry, you're only three centimeters dilated." Holly froze. This couldn't be true. She was rightfully devastated and hopelessly defeated. The doctor continued. "I don't know why the nurse told you that you were at a seven—that is completely unacceptable. I am so, so sorry." Thirty-seven hours in, on the highest dose of Pitocin, with no epidural and no sleep. Finally, in pure agony, sweet Holly joined Team Epidural, and with good fucking reason. After forty-nine hours of labor, little Frankie was born. Holly was able to fully experience the indescribable bliss and was totally in the moment with her ridiculously perfect baby. Holly learned she was even stronger than she ever thought possible—and that sometimes life doesn't go according to plan, and that is okay.

As vivid and cringy as Jill's *South Park* postpartum stories could be, she fully prepared us for the Fourth Trimester. She even dropped off her extra monster pads and perineal spray for me. Thanks, Jill!

Like my birth stories, both of my postpartum experiences were completely different. In general, though, I'd compare the Fourth Trimester to the best/worst drug trip of my life: incredible highs, then debilitating lows. Being drenched in sweat, shaking, hallucinating from sleep deprivation, loopy, giggling for no reason, in a stupid amount of love with someone I just met, tweaked out and constantly paranoid about keeping everyone alive. Often naked with no recollection of how I got that way. Extreme feelings of regret, followed by intense cravings for MORE. There was chaos and bliss, from Nirvana to nervous breakdown within the wipe of an ass. Not to mention my appetite was OFF THE CHAIN; I was stuffing my face more than your favorite character on *My 600-lb. Life*. WAS I THE ONLY ONE WHO COULD NOT STOP EATING?! All I thought about was food (and baby, but FOOD). I went from feeling like a mythical goddess who created a mini-goddess to feeling like a disgusting slime creature who created a gooey crotch goblin. It's basically like being on pure MDMA, except the idea of sex is truly horrific. And then the high wore off and unaliving myself became my latest fantasy. Basically, my postpartum felt like a deleted scene from *Fear and Loathing in Las Vegas*.

If I'm going to compare the postpartum experience with each of my kids, I'd say the physical recovery after Alfie felt like my vag got demolished by a monster truck. While with Poppy, it was more like being hit with a Smart Car. I was physically back to normal so quick with Poppy! Mentally, though, I struggled more the second time. It was understandable, because I had a Hulk-level strong-willed toddler competing for my time and my tit. One minute I was high on fucking fresh air and the indescribably perfect scent of a new baby, followed by a seemingly never-ending emotional roller coaster from the underworld. Bouts of joy followed by a numbingly exhausting vortex that swallowed what was left of my soul. Not to sound dramatic.

When Stephen and I got home from the hospital with Alfie, we were both like, "We're screwed! We'll never sleep again! We'll never watch a movie or have sex!" And we were right. We weren't actually able to have sex for six months. Not six weeks . . . six MONTHS. It's not like I'd vowed celibacy. I had a husband that I (occasionally) wanted to have sex with right there next to me, and I couldn't because my vagina was cock-blocking itself.

I remember going to my six-week checkup with the OB-GYN, the one where the doctor peers inside your battered biscuit to tell you if the war is over, or if the battlefield needs reinforcements. I put my legs in the stirrups, expecting her to recoil and tell me she had never seen such carnage, but instead she was like, "Looks good!" It's shocking to go through childbirth, bleed for weeks, and barely be able to sit down without wincing, only to have someone say, "All clear! NEXT!" So I went home and Stephen and I tried having sex again, and guess what? We could not. After several visits where she'd tell me "*You just need some lube,*" my doctor finally believed me (or maybe she just got tired of inspecting my vagina), and she sent me to a pelvic floor specialist. If you think that sounds like an "L.A. thing," like having a live-in astrologer, pelvic floor therapy is very common in other countries! The French government pays for "perineal reeducation" for women after they give birth. In the U.S. we have to tell a doctor fifteen times that sex feels like a vengeful dagger is stabbing our insides before we can get (non-government) help. America has many freedoms and perks, but pelvic floor therapy is not one of them. If the Constitution had been written by women, things like good pre- and postnatal care and pelvic floor therapy would have FOR SURE been included in the Bill of Rights. I know those Revolutionary mamas could have benefited from some Kegel therapy after all the shit they went through to have their babies. There were no "new mommy" self-care baskets being delivered to their homesteads, and their post-delivery diapers were probably just strips of burlap held together by old chicken wire. There wasn't even AC!

Back in the twenty-first century, all I'd heard about for years was that it was so important for women to do Kegel exercises. If you have not seen *Sex and the City* or you missed the memo about the latest vagina workout craze from twenty-plus years ago, Kegels are a technique that helps strengthen your pelvic floor, and women in real life and on TV (Samantha from *Sex and the City* was VERY into Kegels) were always saying, "Do your Kegels! Don't forget your Kegels!" Jane Fonda even did them in her workout videos. Following in her footsteps, I did a sketch where my Pamela Pupkin character did a Kegel workout video, which basically consisted of Pamela making uncomfortably awkward facial expressions, mixed with even more uncomfortable close-up crotch shots. "Pretend to hold in your pee-for-one-two-three—YUP, hold in your pee-for-one-two-three, now clench your buttocks and release! Ahhhhh..."

Are you doing them right now as I describe it? You totally are! The point is, Kegels are a THING. So imagine my surprise when I waddled into my first session with the pelvic floor therapist and as she peered inside my vagina, she declared, "NO KEGELS FOR YOU!"

I'm sure she said it much more professionally than that, but that was how it sounded to me, like I was being refused soup on *Seinfeld*. At that first session, I cried because it was just all so much. I really felt broken at the time, like there was something wrong with only me. None of my friends had experienced this, or at least none of them talked about it. My therapist ended up being so understanding, helping me see that I wasn't the only woman to have ever experienced a vagina that was closed for business, begrudging and boarded up for many months after giving birth. Were other vaginas as resentful as mine? Was yours? It helped to eventually discover that there were other women who'd experienced the same psychological and physical pain as I was experiencing! Apparently, over 40 percent of women still experience pain during sex six months postpartum. IT'S A GOOD THING BABIES ARE FUCKIN' CUTE.

Like I said, it took me a long time to realize it wasn't just me who had this problem. Most women I knew were back to having sex six or eight weeks after giving birth, but every time Stephen and I tried, I felt immediate sharp pains inside and HAD to stop. Every time my fur-burger came face-to-face with Stephen's doodle-dasher, it immediately screamed in a tough Bronx accent, "WE'RE CLOSED FOR BUSINESS, DICKHEAD! GET OUTTA HERE!"

It reminded me of an experience I'd had years before, when I was in my early twenties and dating a guy named Jake. I was very much in my addiction at that time, and Jake was an addict too, so naturally we bonded over our shared love of drugs and more drugs. Our love language was cocaine and molly and shrooms and vodka and weed. And literally anything else that effectively flooded our brains with feel-good chemicals and numbed us from feeling . . . well . . . anything. Except maybe orgasms? Those were allowed. We were both getting nice-sized paychecks at the time and instead of spending our money on a down payment or putting it in a 401(k), we poured it into our vices. That was our smart way to invest. When investing in magic mushrooms, the return on your investment can be *amaaaazing*. Or terrifying. But there is a CHANCE it will be amazing. Investing is all about ups and downs, and so are mushrooms, so . . . just DM me for any financial questions you have after reading this book, because you will probably have many. The point of this story is, my vagina figured out that this relationship was not healthy for either of us before my brain could catch on.

Out of nowhere, sex with Jake started to become impossible. After several weeks of seducing him and then yelling, "OUCH! STOP!" I started researching and found a condition called *vaginismus*, which is basically painful spasms in the pelvic floor muscles that can make sex or even inserting a tampon excruciating. That was me! Laura Clery, vaginismus sufferer! I felt so seen. There is actually a vaginismus support group on Facebook with over six thousand members, and if I had been on Facebook back in the Jake era, I probably would have become an admin. This was my anti–social media era, though, so I was all alone. I also read that many doctors think vaginismus is caused by psychological fears about sex. Well, duh. Looking back, Jake and I were toxic together, and my addiction was heading to a dark place. So maybe, just maybe, my pelvic floor muscles were trying to protect me. I was also one of those lucky ladies with reoc-curring UTIs, which were often triggered by sex. Sometimes this can be the culprit when it comes to vaginismus. It's your body's way of protecting you from perceived pain. In my case, it was likely a nice combo of the two. So I got some cringy vaginismus therapy DVDs, and I did what every twentysomething woman does when she wants to seduce her lover: I asked Jake to watch them with me.

The DVDs were hosted by an extremely soft-spoken woman named Lilian, who was wearing a flowy pink robe and a yellow statement necklace of giant plastic beads. Once she introduced herself and assured us that she was the vaginismus master, she demonstrated breathing techniques designed to help women and their vaginas relax and open up. The DVD was educational-meets-soft-porn as Lilian breathed heavily, legs spread, and repeated, "Relaaaaaaaax . . . Open your flower . . . ahhhhhhhhh." I tried my best to copy her, but Jake and his penis were an inch away from me, so it was tough. "Dude, I'm getting weirdly turned on by this," Jake muttered. Whether he was turned on by me in my see-through leggings and giant T-shirt (it was 2008, okay?) or by Lilian's dotty-aunt energy is still a mystery.

After days of heavy breathing, my garage finally opened up (with the help of MDMA, which Lilian surprisingly hadn't mentioned), and we had sex again. This went on for a while, but eventually Jake and I broke up because he claimed I was "out of control." When he said that, of course I proceeded to smash a giant painting over his dining room table, causing glass to shatter everywhere. And I was just getting started! I then threw a marble sculpture across the room, which created a hole in his wall. To this day I have no idea why he thought I was "out of control."

It would be years before vaginismus would strike again, this time with Stephen. It was clearly my body's attempt to protect me from my recent physical trauma, meaning pushing an eight-pound, one-ounce baby out my twat. Vaginismus is the body's automatic reaction to the fear of vaginal penetration, and I had a lot of fear and anxiety after giving birth. Giving birth absolutely caused the second shutdown for business, so this time I committed not to the DVDs of Lilian's erotic breathing, but to a plastic penis. Or, to be more accurate, a complement of plastic penises.

Each week, the pelvic floor therapist would gently insert a thingy (medical term) that *looked* like a plastic pencil into my angry vagina. As you relax over time, you graduate to progressively larger vaginal dilators. The first, incredibly skinny plastic pencil thingy reminded me of another ex-boyfriend, who I'll call Brian. Brian had a fancy job in the music industry when we were dating, and he loved to brag about his job and make himself sound like a big shot. He also took great pleasure in putting me down every chance he got. Why my vagina did not Bye, Felicia that guy is beyond me. Maybe it was because his penis was so skinny, my vagina was like, *Fuck it, how much harm can it do while I just take a nap?*

Anyway, Brian was no prince, but I was sort of into him. Okay, not really. I WAS JUST LONELY AND HIGH AND HE WAS JUST THERE. When we were dating, I had just shot this incredible series for AMC called *The Trivial Pursuits of Arthur Banks*. It was with Jeffrey Tambor and Adam Goldberg and I told Brian, "I think it's the best thing I've ever done!"

To which he replied, "It's the ONLY thing you've ever done." Vintage Brian overcompensating for his pencil dick.

He also used to love to ridicule me by telling me I had small breasts, which, according to him, were not appealing to men, ever. But then again, he was dating me AND my tiny tits, so joke's on him! Look, I can go horseback riding and it doesn't even hurt. Boob sweat? I don't know her. There are many perks (pun!) to having titties as flat as Kansas, and thank goodness I had enough psychic defense to see that.

To be fair, I was at the height of my drug career when I was with him, so I was FAR from the perfect girlfriend. Though I never insulted his career or body, and I certainly never called him a pencil dick (to his face). Years later, when I got sober and was going through my Twelve Steps, I called him to make amends for being an unreliable drunk, and he was the only one on my list who didn't forgive me. When I apologized for any harm I had caused, he responded, "No, thank *you*. Seriously. Thanks to you I will NEVER, so LONG as I shall LIVE, date another alcoholic again." Which, fair enough.

A few years after that call, Stephen and I went on a staycation to a romantic hotel on the beach in Santa Monica. We were outside waiting for our car at the valet, holding hands and being all lovey-dovey, like those couples you hate to see when you're single. Suddenly a car pulled up and some guy ran to it and said, "Brian? Are you my Uber driver?"

The driver turned his head and I saw that it was BRIAN, like *Brian* Brian. We locked eyes—this man who bragged to NO END about his prestigious job, who tore me down any chance he could—he was now driving an Uber. Not that there's anything wrong with being an Uber driver! But he was such a pretentious jerk, and he'd always been *so* braggy about his stupid job, it felt like karma.

I turned to Stephen and said, "That was my ex-boyfriend Brian who said my tits were too small for this world."

"What a wanking arsehole!" Stephen said, angry enough to duel over the honor of my tiny tits. I was swooning! Brian drove off and we forgot all about him. We went ahead with our romantic vacation, and I continued feeling wonderful about my appearance AND my life choices.

The reason I bring Brian up at all is because his penis reminded me of the smallest pelvic floor vaginal dilator (plastic pencil thingy). I went to therapy for two months until I graduated to a Stephen-size thingy, which, not to gloat or anything, was the largest size they made. After that, they just stopped, like maybe they were afraid of going too far. Anyway, finally, I'd progressed from Brian to Jake to Stephen-sized, and I was healed. I'm pretty sure I thanked my pelvic floor therapist by sending her a polite email that went something like this:

WE FINALLY PLAYED WITH THE BOX OUR KIDS CAME IN!!!!
Thanks, Vanessa! Hope you had a great weekend. (We did.)

As if the whole barricaded vagina thing wasn't enough torture, after Alfie was born, I was also terrified to poop. Because of the painkillers I was taking, I became uncomfortably constipated— another joy of childbirth. Weeks went by and I hadn't . . . recycled fiber . . . built a log cabin . . . let the turtles loose . . . you know what I mean. My body was so out of whack and I felt so uncomfortable, I was pounding Smooth Move Tea, but nothing worked. My mom suggested I try some laxatives, so I took one and . . . nothing. So she gave me another one. Nothing. So she gave me some more. Always the right dose for laxatives: MORE.

The next day after I took them, I was hurrying to get ready for Alfie's two-week pediatrician appointment. I rushed into the kitchen, threw the diaper bag over my shoulder, and said, "Let's go!"

to Stephen. And then I froze. My eyes grew even bigger than they already are normally.

"Stephen, I . . . I . . . I just . . ."

"What?" he asked, wondering why I was standing there looking like I'd just shit myself.

"I just . . . I . . ."

"Laura! Why are you standing like that?"

I was so mortified and shocked, I couldn't get the words out. Unlike the shit, which had come out no problem.

"What's going on?" Stephen asked.

"You don't want to know . . . you don't want to know . . ." I said, praying this would all turn out to be some nightmarish postpartum fever-dream I would wake from any second. Because I overshare on the internet, some people think Stephen and I are one of those couples who poop in front of each other, but really we're pretty modest when it comes to that stuff. We both grew up in families that never talked about pooping, so we NEVER mention the subject. Except in my books, I guess. It's weird, because there's this totally unnecessary shame attached to it, even though it's the most natural thing ever. I'm actually envious of the couples who can PURPOSELY poop in front of their partners because I could NEVER. Yes, we make videos where we're dancing around in adult diapers together and he's definitely seen me shit myself during childbirth, but that's it! That's where we draw the line.

So anyway, I ran upstairs before he could ask any more questions. "Be right back!"

I quickly (and thoroughly!) cleaned up, changed my clothes, and hurried back downstairs, thankful that the butt tsunami was over.

"Okay, let's go!" I said, hurrying and avoiding eye contact. I felt that if he looked into my eyes, he would have *known* what a literal shit-show I was. We headed out to the car with baby Alfie, and everything seemed great. But then, BOOM! It happened *again*.

"Stephen, I . . . I . . ."

"Yes?"

"I'll be right back!"

It took me weeks to admit to Stephen what had happened, and why I ran/waddled away that morning—TWICE—with terror in my eyes and pants. Even though very few things embarrass me and I make my living doing disconcerting things in public, being a thirty-two-year-old woman who shits herself mid-morning TWICE within twenty minutes seemed like a bridge too far. I had hit soiled bottom. So the lesson here is: Unless your mom is a doctor or nurse, maybe don't listen to her medical advice to take a literal shit-ton of laxatives.

When Alfie was born, my in-laws flew in from England and had front-row seats to me shuffling around in a diaper and spraying milk out of my rock-hard tits. I was in major recovery mode, experiencing my biggest transition in life as a new mom, and there they were, daintily sipping tea. They're the sweetest people ever, and overall I REALLY lucked out in the in-law department . . . but Stephen's dad has never changed a diaper in his entire life and his sweet wife, Mavis, has MS, so that kind of thing is not possible for her anymore. They weren't really in a position to help out. One day I was in the kitchen wearing *my* diaper while also wearing Alfie in a body wrap, while cooking dinner, while cleaning up, while making nonstop teas for everyone in the house (British people really do fucking LOVE tea), and Stephen's mom said very matter-of-factly, "Well, then, you really just get on with it, don't you?"

"Oh, you mean all this," I said gesturing wildly at all the pots and pans I was using while also suffering through vagina pain and swollen breasts and the exhaustion of having about four hours of sleep in the past week. "Well, somebody has to stir the spaghetti sauce, may as well be me! Or Stephen. Or ANYONE ELSE. But I got this!"

Looking back, Stephen's mom felt terrible about not being able to do more. Though she is suffering physically with MS and has been for forty-some years, I've never heard her complain. She remains positive and joyful and as productive as she possibly can be. She really DOES just "get on with it." I am constantly in awe of her for that.

The transition to parenthood wasn't so smooth at first, but it eventually brought Stephen and me even closer . . . to murdering each other. After the initial weeks of chaos and fear and arguing over who changed a diaper last, we developed a routine that kept us from Dextering each other. We traded off mornings with Alfie. On Monday Stephen would take care of him, on Tuesday it was my turn, and we went back and forth so we were equally doing our part. It was a solid system that allowed us each to feel (sort of) rested. The dynamic in our relationship changed so dramatically so fast. We weren't prepared. I was angry that Stephen wasn't getting up at five thirty in the morning to make me a cappuccino so I could breastfeed AGAIN. In AA, I'd learned that expectations are resentments waiting to happen. But like, also, PLEASE MAKE ME A DAMN COFFEE BEFORE I EXPIRE.

My expectation of having foamy oat milk cappuccinos delivered to me on a wooden tray every morning was only one of the reasons we had some fierce fights. It got to the point that Stephen was like, "Laura, I think one kid is enough for us." Shortly after that, when we had figured out a system that worked nicely for both of us, he wanted fifteen more. Now that we are juggling a Tasmanian devil toddler and a six-month-old diva, we've decided two is ENOUGH (we'll see where we stand next month).

Even though I couldn't walk right and was weeping over car commercials, I remember being so madly in love with Alfie. Having a baby truly changed me. For one thing, it made it nearly impossible to be selfish. Which for ME is a big deal. When I was drinking or using, I believe my selfishness was the root cause of most of my problems. I often sat around feeling bad for myself, playing the victim, and obsessing about what I didn't have or what I might lose. It was all about ME, which made me . . . MEEEserable. With my babies around, there ain't no time for that! Sure, sometimes it bummed me out for a minute that I still looked six months pregnant even six months after I'd given birth. But also . . . who fuckin' cares? My body is different now; it's not that important. I thought I'd be like my sisters and go back to having a flat stomach right away, but nope. So what did I do to fix it, you ask? I got pregnant again—genius, I know! This is my body positivity tip for you: If you're feeling bad about the fact that your stomach didn't magically "bounce back," just get pregnant again! Just KEEP getting pregnant. Never stop getting pregnant, ever.

Just like my birth stories, my postpartum with Penelope was very different, but also similar. Partly because I had experienced it before, so I was used to my nipples squirting milk across the room and into a visiting relative's eye. And partly because I wasn't coming down off narcotics. My physical recovery was just SO much better the second time around. And to top it off, my baby-whispering mom was in town and was an amazing help. We also had our incredible nanny Carla, who was on Alfie duty, and Stephen and I had our system down pat. Another reason my second time living through the Fourth Trimester may have been easier (AT FIRST) was that I was eating my own placenta!

Yes, it sounds gross. But if you think about it for even one to two seconds, it IS gross. Yet I'd heard so many women say that taking placenta pills helped them recover quicker during postpartum. I soon became the Los Angeles vegan Hannibal Lecter eating my own afterbirth, which didn't exactly *feel* vegan, but it *was*—because I CONSENTED to being eaten, which no cow has ever done. My placenta nourished my baby for months, so why wouldn't it nourish me? After the horrible way I felt during my first postpartum, I was determined to have a better experience.

I wasn't planning on ingesting my own organ, but a woman who is a "celebrity placenta encapsulation specialist" (it's a thing) reached out to me via Instagram. She wrote a DM along the lines of, "Hey girl! There are so many nutrients in a woman's placenta. Wanna eat yours!?" It took me a while to reply. I wasn't trying to be rude, but it didn't feel like a snap decision either. Eventually, after about the fifteenth DM, I said, "Fuck it! I'll try some placenta." Even if it was a placebo effect, who cares?

After Poppy was born and we shipped this woman my organ (deepest apologies to USPS!), she sent us an unsolicited video of the encapsulation process. Maybe because it's not FDA approved (red flag?) and she wanted us to see that the processing was not being done in a dark basement in Siberia? The video is one of those sped-up time-lapse tabletop shots, so it's kind of like you're watching a cute DIY crafting video on TikTok. Except instead of watching someone process cute tissue-paper flowers for a festive spring wreath, it's the bloody tissue from my slimy placenta. She wore hot-pink gloves and added an upbeat techno soundtrack. If you didn't know what you were looking at, you might think Björk was making spaghetti. Once the blood ran down the drain and she dried the placenta, she stuffed it into pills. Every time I took a pill I heard phantom techno music, but I was willing to try anything to feel better than the first time around. I still can't tell you whether I healed faster the second time around because I went unmedicated or because I was eating my own organ, but I do know that I had more energy and I didn't need to use a donut cushion every time I sat down.

A couple of weeks in, I stopped taking the pills, because honestly they started to disgust me. On the third day without the pills, I had my worst day of postpartum since Poppy was born. I was feeling really down and also couldn't sleep for the life of me, so I decided to put my placenta back into my mouth. Swallowing something revolting sounded better than *feeling* revolting.

When the celebrity placenta lady sent me the pills, she also included a watercolor print made with my placenta. It was very thoughtful/creepy. She'd also made a gold heart out of Poppy's umbilical cord, so at the end of the day I guess she is a crafter? I will say I've gotten a lot of joy out of placing the creepy print on Stephen's pillow to scare him at night. Maybe one day he'll appreciate it. Maybe in our old age we'll die in bed together like they did in *The Notebook,* each with one hand on our placenta watercolor.

One postpartum side effect that cannot be cured by pills, no matter how disgusting their contents, is mom brain. I had just been through a life-changing, sometimes joyous, always exhausting experience. I had a new *human being* I was responsible for plus a strong-willed and nonverbal toddler competing for my milk wagons, and I was getting little sleep. How was I supposed to remember my own name or what year I was living in? I didn't! Mom brain is real, and it's kinda like being stoned out of your mind, minus the "high." I was just dumber, hungrier, and had random delirious laughing fits over baby farts. You know, there are scientific studies that show that the gray matter in a woman's brain *actually shrinks* after childbirth so she can cope with her extreme new circumstances. A father's brain does not shrink, so he can keep composing meditation music and waxing his car as nature intended. But moms? We are reduced to pea-brains. The cool thing is, the shrinkage actually helps us bond with our babies and understand their nonverbal cues, so our brains may get smaller, but we get more emotionally intelligent. My favorite part of one of the studies said that scientists do not yet know whether the effects are permanent or temporary. In my experience so far, they have been permanent.

In a way, I've been training for mom-brain shrinkage FOR YEARS.

Back in my twenties, I dated and lived with a nice, supportive German guy named Rudolf (who you might remember from my first book). He was super healthy and he got me to do yoga at the Jewish senior center nearby. For two dollars a class IT WAS A STEAL. He was one of the few people I dated at that time who was even remotely a good influence—he was also twenty years older than me. Daddy issues much? Anyway, the thing he could not teach me how to do was to stop drinking and doing drugs. That was on me.

So one night Rudolf was out with a friend and I was sitting home alone, smoking a lot of pot. Suddenly there was a loud knock at the door. It was after 9 p.m. and I knew it wasn't Rudolf, so I panicked. We lived near a sketchy park in West Hollywood where crackheads and dealers hung out, so I held my breath, shut my eyes, and willed the evil person banging on the door to leave. But there it was again. BAMBAMBAM! This person (or people—it could have been a whole gang of murderers!) was pounding on the door, so I of course thought, *That's it! I'm going to get raped and murdered, or murdered and then raped!* I ran into the bathroom, locked the door, got into the bathtub, and called Rudolf.

"I'm about to get murdered!" I whisper-screamed. "There's someone pounding on the door! It's probably a rapist! Or several rapists! Or it's ALL the rapists in L.A., together?"

"I will be right there, Laura!"

The pounding continued. I knew this was it for me.

I waited in the tub because nothing bad ever happens in horror movies in the bathroom (except in *Psycho, The Shining, Poltergeist, Nightmare on Elm Street* and *Ghoulies*! Also in *Fatal Attraction* and *Arachnophobia* and *Scream 2* and *Final Destination*!). Anyway, my brain had spun out beyond my control. I could barely even remember why I was in the tub. I was so scared that I started to doze off. Eventually, Rudolf knocked on the door, and I let him in, falling into his arms. He had saved me from being mutilated by a mob of sadistic serial killers!

"I don't see anyone, Laura," he said in his thick German accent. "There is no one there."

"Oh my God," I said, my brain suddenly putting together a few hazy puzzle pieces.

"What is it?" said Rudolf.

"Shit," I said.

"What is it?"

"I think . . ."

"Yes, Laura?"

61

"Okay, yeah. I don't think there was a gang of murderers at the door. I think . . . I ordered a pizza and then forgot? Yeah, no, I definitely ordered a medium thin-crust. It was the pizza guy knocking, not Ted Bundy."

So you see, my old brain on drugs was pretty much the same as my new-mom brain. In both cases my mind basically malfunctions, I forget everything, I don't trust my own thoughts, and I'm a walking, grunting, paranoid, hungry idiot for most of the day (and night). It's actually a miracle that women can function at all during the Fourth Trimester. I may forget my name or the names of the babies I just birthed, but somehow I still get shit done. Just like Stephen's mom said to me: "You just get on with it, don't you?" Yes, I do! What other choice do I have? Leave everything behind and take a plane to the farthest reaches of Western Samoa and never show my face again? Run away to Paris and become a mime? Disappear into the Brazilian rain forest and live off the land? Damn, that all sounds so relaxing, actually. If I don't post any videos for a while, I MIGHT be in one of those places, but don't come looking for me!

When I was in my addiction, it was all about do-re-me-me-me-me-me-MEEE! I was riddled with a thousand forms of fear—that I would lose what I had or never get what I wanted. Years into my sobriety I realized that untreated alcoholism (or any untreated addiction) is a literal recipe for misery. There's a great documentary called *Happy* where the filmmakers travel around to the happiest places on earth and ask people HOW THE FUCK DO YOU DO IT?!! But in a nicer way. It comes down to things like self-growth (loving and becoming yourself), having meaningful relationships (loved ones), and being of service (contributing to a better world). No wonder I was so depressed in my addiction! Addicts are notorious isolators (no connection), selfish and self-seeking to the extreme (no service work), and crippled by fear (no self-growth). When I learned to live sober, I slowly learned to love myself, reach out, and give back. I learned to walk through my fear rather than attempt to numb it, even though life can be scarier than the video of my placenta being mashed up. Working the Twelve Steps and trying to live by those principles healed me. More than ten years later, after struggling with relapse early on and working to stay sober again, here I am. Currently a delirious mess in spit-up-stained sweatpants, but I'm still sober, bitch!

Both times during postpartum, I felt that same kind of isolation that I felt in my addiction. I found myself not wanting to see friends or even FaceTime with them. I mean, I was sitting there leaking out of my nipples, forehead, armpits, and poontang, I'd had no sleep, and I was attached to a crying baby (and then babies), so entertaining guests was not at the top of my list. I even cancelled on my lifelong friend Jack when he wanted to meet Penelope, and he was my partner in crime with whom I could be 100 percent myself. I was just too concerned about the chaos, feeling like I'd rather not be social. But reaching out, even if it was just joining group texts with friends, saved me. Just like with recovery, seeing others and being vulnerable is always healing. It reminded me that whether you're battling mom brain or depression or feeling like a train wreck after having a baby, reaching out to someone will help—none of us can do it alone. Unless you take too many laxatives, in which case you probably *should* be alone for a while, in the bathroom with the door locked. But other than that one corner case, it takes a village.

Just when I thought I had things under control after Poppy was born, I fell into a pretty deep postpartum depression. I cried into a newborn diaper (don't give me that look—it was clean!); I had morbid thoughts; I fought with Stephen. My mind was becoming a scary place. I had moments of indescribable bliss followed by a horrible sense of dread in the pit of my stomach . . . and then feelings of guilt for even feeling sad at all. I was so blessed, after all. How selfish and lazy was I to cry when I had just birthed a perfectly healthy and beautiful baby? My baby didn't even have an ugly phase, it was ridiculous! Then, of course, I felt I had to hide my struggle. I was becoming so exhausted but still unable to sleep. When I finally did sleep, I'd wake up drenched—not damp, but drenched, head to toe—with sweat. Apparently, my estrogen had fled to Western Samoa without me. But then, just as I was feeling disgusting drenched in all that sweat, I'd look into my baby's eyes as she fed from my hard and swollen breasts and I'd just feel so in love. The bliss would be back in full force.

———

Until it wasn't.

One day after another fight with Stephen, I sort of "hit bottom." I felt like I'd been sitting across from myself, *watching myself* go insane. I was shifting from positivity to morbidity within the change of a diaper. My thoughts ran rampant: *Why is my right breast stupidly larger than my left? This is temporary, right?? My body feels strained . . . as does my relationship. We're having zero sex. There's too much arguing. Didn't "they" say having kids made you closer? I'm scared Stephen will leave me for someone more fun. I'm not fun right now. And I feel fugly. Do people still say "fugly"? Yet another reminder that I'm getting old. I've lost touch with SLANG (gasp), which means I'm closer to my death! Oops . . . there goes the morbidity . . . Or was that positivity, because sometimes I want to die. I want to end it all but I can't. I can't do that to my babies. They need me. OR . . . maybe they would be better off with someone more maternal? Someone who knows how to crochet and who doesn't say "fuck" all the time?*

One day, as the torrent of thoughts went through my brain, I told my mom I needed to run to the store quickly and asked if she could watch the little ones. I drove with tears in my eyes to Whole Foods. HOW MUCH DO I SOUND LIKE A KAREN RIGHT NOW? I sat in the parking lot and straight up broke DOWN. My eyes were soaked and my nose was running. I looked around for a napkin or paper towel and found nothing until I shamelessly blew my nose into a diaper and thought, *I can't be alone in this. I CAN'T be the only one feeling this way.* I decided I was sick of going through it alone, and that I should just make a video, right then and there, asking other moms if they had experienced all of the guilt, shame, and sadness I had been feeling five weeks into having a new baby.

When I posted about it, thousands of women responded with their own stories of mental and physical pain, paranoia, and depression after having babies. As much as I hate it that they struggled too, it was a beautiful thing to see the conversation happening. Turns out feeling validated and understood was one of the most effective weapons in my battle against PPD. There were literally thousands of women getting so vulnerable in the comments and assuring me that I WAS NOT ALONE. It was so healing for me and hopefully for so many others. I was a bit apprehensive about posting that postpartum video because I figured some people might say, "You're successful, Laura, you have nothing to be depressed about!" And what do you know . . . some did.

One woman even responded to my video with about twenty

TikTok rants telling me I had no business being depressed because I was sort-of famous. She mocked me for having "an au pair and going to Mommy and Me sessions." Her overall message was how dare I complain about depression or anxiety or motherhood, since I had . . . money. First of all, I've never been to a Mommy and Me session—they sound like my idea of hell. Second of all, I had to google "What is an au pair?" And third, comparative suffering has literally never helped anyone ever. Just because someone has success or money doesn't mean they don't struggle. Look at Anthony Bourdain, Robin Williams, Whitney Houston, Amy Winehouse, and so many others.

To be very clear, it's not lost on me that I am extraordinarily blessed in my life. But unfortunately, career, money, and social status account for only 10 percent of my personal happiness (pretty low), and the other 90 percent can be a real bitch. Money and fame haven't cured my alcoholic and depressive genes or my ADHD. Another thing they discovered in the "Happy" doc was that if you go from homeless to having food and shelter, your happiness level rises significantly, but after you have your needs met, and your money goes up, your happiness level does not. Basically saying, so long as your basic needs are met, MORE MONEY WILL NOT BUY HAPPINESS. And it certainly won't protect you from PPD. And I actually *do* know what it's like to struggle financially, as I've spent much more of my life broke than not. I fully acknowledge how blessed I am these days to be able to buy the chia seed almond butter, but that doesn't change my genes or wash away my challenges.

Despite the pushback, getting vulnerable and posting myself breaking down in the grocery store parking lot while blowing my nose into a diaper was one of the best decisions I had ever made. It not only helped me to heal and feel less alone, but it also started an IMPORTANT and NEEDED conversation. Too many women, including myself, felt ashamed for feeling the way we did, and too many women suffer silently. It was one of the most liberating experiences to connect with so many women on such a deep level, with all of us sharing openly and honestly about our struggles. So yeah, a shout-out to all the women who commented about their extremely personal struggles on a public platform. That's not easy to do. But only through talking about it together, and not tearing each other down, will things ever improve.

I wish more people talked about the ups and downs of parenting, and about what it's *really* like. Maybe the shame and guilt would lessen if we all openly acknowledged how hard it is. And gratifying . . . and painful . . . and blissful . . . and excruciating . . . and exhilarating . . . and frustrating . . . and fun. It is all of those things, plus a million more. I asked myself recently what I would tell my children if I saw them suffering the way that I was during my PPD. I'd tell them *not* to stay silent. I'd tell them to speak up and that it's absolutely nothing to be ashamed of. I'd tell them they are perfect as they are. Plus, it's progress, not perfection. I'd tell them that we can overcome anything and that they are always 100 percent unconditionally loved no matter what.

Maybe you are one of the lucky ones who never experienced the positivity/morbidity roller coaster from hell. Or maybe you're scared and ashamed of what people will think of you if you admit that you, too, wrestle with darkness. Like it somehow means you don't love your kids as much . . . But I know that you do! Or that by openly struggling, you're somehow not grateful for all you do have . . . But I know that you are! If this is you . . . please tell someone. Anyone.

Everyone! Fuck the stigma! Fuck the shame! We can get through this together. We are not alone.

Besides the dark thoughts and the recurring night sweats, not being able to have sex for SIX MONTHS after Alfie was born had traumatized me. So when I went to my six-week checkup after Poppy was born, I was once again shocked when my doctor peeped in my vagina and said, "Everything looks good! Next . . ."

Especially since I had been walking around feeling like my uterus was making its way downward and would soon just fall out onto the curb while I was taking my daily walk. It was a strange feeling. Different from last time. This time, I felt a sort of heaviness in my pelvis. It really only bothered me when I went for long walks. It wasn't painful at all. It just felt . . . almost swollen? I called my doctor and told her that I felt like something was wrong, like, I don't know, my vagina was broken? AGAIN. She said, "Want to VagTime me?"

"You mean FaceTime," I suggested.

"No, VagTime."

So she wanted to look at my vagina, on the app that's helped countless grandparents stay connected to their fidgety grandkids? The app you use when you want to show someone the new gazebo you installed out back. She wanted to video chat with the kitty cat.

Many people would answer her question with, "No thanks and goodbye," or "Are you fucking kidding me," but I said:

"Is ANYONE around you? Anyone at all? Colleagues? Kids? ABC News? Your dog? Are you in a Starbucks with a creepy stranger trying to look over your shoulder?"

"No," she said coolly. "VagTime me."

"You're sure NO ONE IS AROUND YOU?"

"It's VagTime," she said.

So I did. I DID.

She "examined" my vagina—THROUGH AN iPHONE—and said she thought she saw a tiny cyst.

"Hold on, let me screenshot it and zoom in to make sure . . ."

"Could you not? I don't want my vagina to end up starring in a medical TikTok. I'm all for putting my life out there for people to see, but NOT the inside of my bajingo."

"Okay, come in tomorrow," she said as I pulled up my sweats and we wrapped up our VagTime. "It just looks like a little cyst. Take sitz baths and have sex, and I'll see you tomorrow."

What the . . . fuck? Having sex was the thing I could NOT do, and she was prescribing it as a remedy? I could barely walk down the hall.

The next day at the appointment she looked at my actual vagina, in person, and again she said, "Looks fine to me. Next!"

"Are you SURE?"

"Yep! All good. You wanna see?" She handed me a mirror so I could examine as well.

"Okay . . . so yeah . . . I see a little skin tag there but, what about THAT thing?" I pointed to a small bulge above the opening of my vagina . . .

She looked at me like I was a fucking idiot.

"That's your urethra. You know—where your pee comes out?"

"Right. Okay. Yeah. No, I knew that. Totally. I just don't remember it being there."

"Okay . . ." she said, looking more and more done with me by the minute.

There was an awkward pause as I continued to thoroughly examine my vagina as if I were seeing it for the first time.

"What about that? What's that?" I pointed to another . . . area.

"That's your inner labia."

"Yeah, I know. I know. I was just checking your knowledge. So . . ."

Another long pause followed. I attempted to fill the silence.

"Vaginas are crazy, right?"

She got up. "Okay, well, I have another patient. So, if you need to VagTime me again, just let me know."

"Will do!"

When I got home, I immediately started googling my symptoms. I understand Google does not have a medical degree, but I have very little self-control and something still wasn't adding up.

After five minutes of research, I had a diagnosis: pelvic organ prolapse. I had never heard of it, but apparently over THREE MIL-LION women in the U.S. suffer from this. Why don't more people talk about it? Women joke about peeing themselves after childbirth, but really they should be saying, "I'm one of the THREE MILLION women who suffer from uterine prolapse, which is why I pee myself in restaurants now. Pass the salt!" Our health-care system is tragic. If men experienced this, it would have been put on insurance plans a century ago.

After about four weeks of feeling this way, I was pretty devastated. Between that, my relationship being strained, my mind and my body being mushy, and having no sleep, I was not in a good place. I hosted an epic pity party for one in my bed. Only my giant nursing pads got an invite. Then I became obsessed with googling every configuration of "pelvic organ prolapse" you can think of and it became my whole world. My pelvic floor therapist did eventually confirm that I had a Grade 1 prolapse. My Google searches had been more reliable than my doctor, which is a statement that should horrify everyone.

I felt broken: mentally, physically, and spiritually. One day, Stephen and I were touring a preschool for Alfie, and the school director asked me if I was okay, which tells you how not okay I must have looked. I just broke down in tears. You know you're in a bad place when you start weeping just because someone asks, "Hey, how's your day?" What I wanted to say was, "Not great, because I'm pretty sure my rectum is attempting to escape from my vag." But instead I just wiped my tears and said, "Oh, are these the monkey bars?"

Eventually, I couldn't take it anymore. I mean my mental state, but also the preschool tour. I was done. I was so sick and tired of feeling sick and tired. I decided I would do whatever I had to do to stop feeling like a bag of dicks.

In the following days, I forced myself to take all my vitamins, drink more water and slightly less coffee, and reach out to my friends. I started meditating again, if only for three minutes at a time, and if I ever felt myself slipping, I would basically WILL MYSELF into positivity. It's not that I was ignoring my feelings—quite the opposite. I had dwelled in the darkness for TOO long and I was DONE. My morning walks were also incredibly crucial in helping me pull myself out of my depression. I'd done enough "feeling my feelings and sitting in my pain." I wanted out. I was determined to focus on what I WANTED rather than what I didn't want. So, every time I started having intrusive thoughts or dwelling on my imperfect marriage or the fact that my organs were trying to escape my body, I would just *obsessively* repeat, "I'm so happy and grateful that I'm healthy and my kids are healthy and my marriage is stronger than ever and so is my pelvic floor." I would spend time every day getting grateful for all the good in my life and then visualizing what I wanted, which was to feel healthy, happy, loving, energetic, and creative. I was determined to love myself fully once again, remove my fear, and replace it with love. Every time I had a shitty thought, I would challenge myself to counter it with a nice one. I do believe that pain can be the touchstone of mental growth and that if we look hard enough, there is a spiritual lesson in even our most painful moments. Obviously this journey looks different for everyone, but I can tell you that within about a week or two of totally prioritizing my mental health, my depression started lifting. And guess what? So did my internal organs. Now, I don't think it's magic. I think it's as simple as instead of me obsessively googling horror stories about organs escaping asses, I CHOSE to watch ONLY success stories of women who had recovered. I did what they did. I visualized healing. I believed it was possible. I stayed in the solution and stopped dwelling in the problem. I also tried to practice acceptance: accepting the reality of my life as it was in that moment and then having the courage to do something about it. I practiced unconditionally valuing *all* parts of me (progress, not perfection) and then somehow mustered up the courage to change what I could. I know, this is easier said than done. But when I finally started to crawl out of the Fourth Trimester–induced fatalistic gloom and started to see the light . . . man, what a gift!

CHAPTER 3

The Accidental Lactivist

*Lactivism (noun): strong advocacy of breastfeeding (sometimes used
with negative connotation, suggesting an uncompromising approach)*

I was a late bloomer. Not in height, because I was basically in the
thousandth percentile at birth, but when it came to puberty, I was
last to the party. A tiny speck in a universe of boobs. I didn't actually
catch up until I reached my thirties and had a baby, which is when
my boobs filled out (and up). That's when I finally transformed into
every man's dream: a grown woman leaking milk into huge nipple pads.

I remember one day back in fifth grade, I was sitting on a lime-
green beanbag reading the Goosebumps classic *You Can't Scare Me*.
A kid named Bryan Frizell walked over, and I peered up from my
book. I assumed he was going to tell me he was in love with me, or
at least ask what book I was reading. Instead, he looked straight at
my chest and said, "It's like looking at a wall."

How long had Bryan been practicing that line? Or did it just
come to him fully formed when he walked up? It was so stupid, but
I'm sure he thought that it cut deep, and it did. All the girls' chests

were walls at that age, but I guess I was the flattest wall of them all. I don't have a fantastic memory for most things, but I will never forget what Bryan Frizell did that day. It deeply humiliated me at the time. At least his comment gave me thicker skin (but unfortunately not thicker tits).

I've come a long way since the day I was sitting on that beanbag. It was a journey that took me from a zero cup ALL THE WAY to a B cup. It was a journey that involved two births, hours of breast-feeding and pumping, and countless letdowns, both psychological and actual milk "let-downs." I wish I could find Bryan and tell him that people LOVE my boobs now. "People" meaning my two children and my husband! Actually, now it's just Poppy and Stephen, since Alfie finally, reluctantly, agreed to let his baby sister take over. But only after he put up a valiant fight, many times, until finally he granted his sister sole custody of my milk jugs.

As a teenager I was a 34A (with the help of t.p. stuffed in my bra), but as an adult I blossomed to a 34B. Having small breasts never bothered me—without massive sweater-stretchers in my way, I could fit into narrow spaces like my first L.A. apartment. It was an apartment made for ants. Okay, maybe that's an exaggeration; it was actually an apartment made for leprechauns. Seriously, though, I had to duck my head to get into my own bathroom. I looked like the Hunchback of Notre Dame every time I had to pee. I also couldn't stand up in my own bedroom. I called it "the cave" because it was literally a cave. It was on the top floor of the building and I'm pretty sure the landlord converted it from the attic into another apartment—which is why I COULDN'T FIT IN IT. It was definitely not up to code, BUT IT WAS CHEAP! Tiny and cheap. Or as they say in real estate, a "charming steal" charmingly stole my vertebra health forever.

Okay, back to my milk wagons.

I was good with my 34Bs until I had a boyfriend who one day said, "Dude, I wish your boobs were bigger. All guys like big tits."

"Some guys like smaller breasts," I said, standing up for flat-chested women everywhere.

"That's not a thing," he said, before he went back to his bong.

It *is* a thing, though, because I ended up finding and marrying a man who likes my breasts. Stephen is more of an ass man (both in that he can be an ass and he also prefers them), but little did he know that once we had kids, I would turn into the milk-fountain goddess of my ex-boyfriend's dreams.

If you ask me what my bra size is now, I'll tell you I joggle (jug-toggle) between a 36-I-D-F-K (I Don't Fucking Know) and a 36-D-O-T-D (Depends On The Day). My size actually depends on the TIME of day. Some mornings my boobs are two giant hot-air balloons stuck to my rib cage, and by midday they're more like two . . . normal-size hot-air balloons stuck to my rib cage. They have gone totally rogue and I have no control over how they look or what they do at any given moment. Their attitude reminds me of myself in my early twenties. Completely unpredictable, with a lot of hard days. Some days they're so lopsided, I refer to them as "Biggie Smalls" and I proceed to recite the lyrics to "Mo Milk, Mo Problems."

The more tit milk I come across, the fatter baby beeeeeee!!!

Breastfeeding is not for the weak. If you think my ex-boyfriends sound scary, you have not experienced the terror of sticking your nipple inside a teething baby's mouth. Back in my early twenties, I never imagined that I would be tied down to one boyfriend or man, let alone be at the mercy of not one but two small people who used my boobs as their own personal all-you-can-eat buffet. I was very lucky, though, that I had a good supply and Alfie was immediately hooked. Literally.

Alfie was one of those babies that basically crawled up immediately after birth, found a boob, and ransacked the smorgasbord. When it happened, my nerves went away and I just thought it was cool that I was keeping another human alive with my slammers! It felt magical, powerful, and beautiful, so I posted photos of it. I wasn't trying to make some big statement or become a lactivist (a.k.a. a staunch breastfeeding advocate). I was just living life and thinking, "Breastfeeding is awesome! Why did no one tell me how cool this was?!"

It became part of my daily—okay, hourly—life. I wasn't skydiving or lounging by a pool; I was runnin' the boob buffet, twenty-four hours a day, straight from the tap. I got out of bed, he breastfed; I ate breakfast, he ate breast-fast; I took a nap, he took a nip; I woke up, he soaked up—you get it. I make content about my life, and breastfeeding became my life. I felt exhausted and over it at times, but overall, I'm one of those weirdos who loves to breastfeed. I LOVE the bonding experience. I LOVE the way it makes me feel. Maybe it's because I'm an ex–drug addict and I craved that hit of oxytocin, the hormone that chills me the EFF out and makes me not want to chuck my baby out the window. Breastfeeding was magical for me. And when I learned about all of its benefits for the baby, like providing antibodies that help babies fight off viruses and bacteria (among MANY more benefits), well, even better! So, I posted about it. Some people cheered my openness about breastfeeding—but some, not so much. I was actually shocked at the absolute outrage that ensued after a harmless post of me feeding my baby. Look, if you don't want to see my milk wagons, unfollow. WHY IS THIS SUCH A BIG DEAL? Oh, I know! It's because our culture has made it a big deal. Should I not feed my hungry baby in public JUST IN CASE there is some sick pervert watching? What about the weirdo with a foot fetish? Are you never going to wear flip-flops? Whether it's in a dark room or a bright restaurant with children around, at the end of the day, breastfeeding is a woman's right!

How could I know that breastfeeding would piss so many people off? There were tons of supporters, but then there was the anti-boob army. As soon as I started sharing photos, the army started lobbing grenades at my ta-tas, and their outrage truly baffled me. Oh, and most of them were WOMEN! They would comment that the photos were inappropriate or that I was just seeking attention. Talk about internalized misogyny! Oh, and then there were the "There are children using this app, how dare you!" comments. Out of the millions of things on social media that are corrupting children, a photo of a mother nursing a baby is not one of them.

When Alfie was about six months old, Stephen and I were having lunch at one of our favorite French cafés in Los Angeles, Le Pain Quotidien. I have never been able to pronounce it and probably never will, but they have delicious bread. Is it Luh-Pain-Quotiden? Ley-Pin-Ti-Dien? Is the *Q* always silent? Is *Q* never silent? Why didn't I pay more attention in French class?!

I was having a lentil salad, and Alfie was having my tit. True multitasking is feeding yourself while also feeding another human *from your own body* while holding a conversation while not peeing yourself. It's a juggling act . . . with your jugs. Stephen thought it was cute that Alfie and I were having lunch together, so he posted about it, with a scandalous caption like "Aww, they're both eating lunch." It was a sweet moment for us. We were first-time parents, completely in love with our then six-month-old son. To top off the sweetness, this same restaurant was where Stephen and I had our very first date! I remember we sat there for over three hours, getting to know each other and laughing a lot in the process. Now, seven years later, we were back, with a whole other human. Who would have thought?! It was also one of the first times we had left our home to eat at a restaurant as a family of three. It was an amazing feeling, so we wanted to share that.

And then, out of the blue, one woman became Le Pain in My Ass.

Responding to the Instagram story of me feeding our son, this stranger sent me a DM:

> U have no self-respect for yourself feeding that child like that. No dignity towards urself.
> U should be shamed of urself. Hes too big for ur boibs. Feed your husband ur boibs.

In case you think everyone involved in the production of this book forgot how to use spell-check, the woman actually kept writing "boibs" instead of "boobs." She didn't misspell it this way once, she misspelled it this way every single time she wrote it. Stephen and I thought it was absolutely appalling and absolutely hilarious. So naturally, I posted a screenshot of her message to millions of people along with my reply:

> No self-respect for feeding my 6-month-old hungry baby? I am happily willing to be stared at & judged just to nourish my baby. I'd say that's pretty dignified. & Would YOU want to eat with a blanket

over your head?? So why should my baby have to? Oh, & breasts
were made to feed babies. My husband is good with almond milk.
I'm not breaking the law, it's my choice, & you can fuck off.

The thread went viral, with thousands of women sharing their
own stories of being shamed for breastfeeding. They talked about
the dirty looks and comments and judgment they had experienced,
and for the first time I fully realized what an important issue this was.
I started seeing the #normalizebreastfeeding hashtag and realizing
that I was far from the only one being told to put my boibs away. I
also posted a response video laying out all the hate comments I had
gotten about breastfeeding. One of my favorites was the old zinger
about Alfie being too old, to which I replied, THERE IS NO SUCH
THING AS AN OLD BABY!

Because there's not. Except Benjamin Button, who does not count.

I took action. I called out the haters on their own shit and reminded
people that breasts are not on women so that *Playboy* or *Maxim* can
have marketable covers. At the dawn of time they didn't even HAVE
Playboy and *Maxim*! They had cave-drawing porn, probably.

This all happened around the same time we were approached to
start a clothing line. Stephen and I had been up at night, struggling
to come up with a name for the brand. Our business partners were
adamant that we not call the brand *Laura Clery*. Their logic was that
just because people like my comedy does not mean they want to buy
my sweatpants. And I get that. One time I saw a pair of sunglasses
I liked at T.J.Maxx, but when I saw a celebrity name written on
the side, I just COULD NOT bring myself to buy them. So I get
it. Who knows, if I named my clothing brand *Laura Clery*, would
people flash back to the time I wrote a song called "Buttholes Are

Nothing to Be Laughed At" and then not want to buy my maternity bra? It's frighteningly possible.

So, Stephen and I had been racking our brains for a name, but we were hitting a wall flatter than my fifth-grade chest. During that time, we traveled from L.A. to Oregon to visit my sister Colleen and her family on their eighty-acre farm. The playscape for their kids is a giant tree stump, they grow their own heirloom tomatoes and kale, and they LOVE to discuss permaculture and ecosystems. Preserving the natural environment and harvesting local crops is really important, you guys, but more important was the fact that we still hadn't thought of a good name for our brand! My sister and her husband live like it's 1873, making coffee using this manual coffee grinder that takes a fortnight to make a single cup. My brother-in-law says that electric grinders compromise the integrity of the beans, and he can fuck right off with whatever it is that's keeping me from drinking A CUP OF COFFEE. Every morning Stephen and I would wait impatiently, aging into our winter years as those beans got ground up, while Colleen was off playing her guitar and singing in French. So we woke up one morning in our quaint farmhouse room, freezing our twenty-first-century asses off (because apparently, using heat is bad for the environment). We were dreading the coffee grinder debacle but, admittedly, loving our artisanal sheets made by blind Tibetan monks. Then, Stephen popped up in our Victorian cot and yelled, "I've got it!"

"A triple-shot cappuccino from Starbucks?!" I asked hopefully.

"The name of the clothing brand!"

"Oh," I said, disappointed. Don't people know nothing matters before coffee?

"We'll call it . . . BOIBS!"

I stared at Stephen, who was beaming with pride beneath a locally sourced, handwoven Guatemalan wall hanging.

"That's the worst idea I've ever heard," I said as gently as I could.

"Is it the *worst* idea," Stephen asked a little maniacally, ". . . OR IS IT THE BEST?"

Fifteen hours later, we received our coffee. Meanwhile, I'd had some time to think about the name Boibs. It started to develop and grow on me, and I realized that Stephen was right. It might just be . . . perfect. I loved that it is a nonsense word, like Goop or Yeezy. It's catchy and fun, and it has a meaningful origin story. A clothing brand inspired by the spelling error of a troll?! Was this genius or insane? Or both? As we finished our coffee, I agreed and signed off, and Boibs was born.

My dream for this brand is to make affordable products with a sense of humor. I noticed all the other "mom" brands are so precious. There's nothing really edgy or funny about them. They paint motherhood with an excessively refined filter, and it just doesn't speak to me or my followers. Boibs is for the mom and dad who love to cuddle their angelic baby, but at one point may have tried heroin. Or for the mom who loves nothing more than reading a bedtime story to her child, but who also says things like, "Another fucking blowout, how can I return to sender??" It's for the perfectly imperfect person who doesn't try to act like they have their shit together. A family-wear brand for the not-so-typical family. I realized how crucial it is to have a sense of humor when raising a family, and I couldn't find any cool clothing brands that were actually affordable for young, eccentric, irreverent families like us . . . and so began the birth of Boibs.

I guess I could have "been the bigger person" and ignored the hate comment, but in this case I am so glad I didn't. If someone puts you down, you can ignore them and be the bigger person OR you can blast their comment to millions and create a clothing line out of their spelling error. Turn their mistake into your success. In the same way they turned your beautiful boobs into boibs, we can turn boibs into the beautiful brand Boibs.

———

Somehow, people saw my posts and decided I was on a one-woman mission to convince millions of people that breastfeeding was the only way—but I'm more of an accidental lactivist. It's each woman's choice how she wants to feed her baby, and not all women are actually able to breastfeed. However you feed your kid is none of my business! But just by reading so many horrible comments, I became outraged by all the judgment and ridicule that women face for breastfeeding. It became important to me over time, and I DO care about this issue. Also, if I'm breastfeeding 75 percent of the time, and I vlog about my real life, it would be a little weird not to show it, right? Would you rather watch me sleeping? Because when I'm not breastfeeding, I'm probably sleeping. There is very little that happens in-between.

I never took a class on breastfeeding or on anything birth- or parenting-related. I just YouTubed how to deal with engorgement or leaking through your shirt while you're in a meeting or putting silicone suction cups on your boobs, which is *just* as relaxing as it sounds. As if all those things were not scandalous enough, people also got angry at me because I was tandem feeding a newborn *and* a toddler. Some people declared that Alfie was "too old" or that he was taking precious milk away from Penelope. Then there are other women commenting how strong I am for feeding them both—but really I'm just very bad at saying no. I sometimes *wanted* to say no, and I tried every trick, but boobs solve all problems. They're the ultimate peacemakers.

Right after Alfie turned two, I tried to start weaning him from the peacemakers, but he was not having it. The poor kid had hoarded them all to himself for two years. Why should he just wave a white flag and give them up to this eight-pound stranger squatting unin-vited in his house? And because I am a people pleaser who cannot say "no," I would give in to him time and time again. I mean . . . he's really cute. Finally, when I had no soul left because it had been sucked out through my tits by my children, I called my sister Colleen and asked her what I should do. She generously took a break from strumming an Edith Piaf classic and watering her garden of ancient grains to answer.

"Just gently explain to him that his sister needs the milk to survive and get her nutrients. That's what I did, and it worked right away."

I thanked Colleen, hung up the phone, and immediately told Stephen that my sister was delusional and living in 1873, and that she told me to just ASK HIM TO STOP. Stephen and I cracked up at Colleen's ridiculous LIES. I then called my mom to tell her what Colleen had said, and even my MOM laughed and thought it was ridiculous and impossible and VERY VICTORIAN. Well, the joke was on all of us except for Colleen, because finally, one day, I looked Alfie in the eyes and said, "You know, your sister needs all this milk to get the nutrients so she can grow . . ." And suddenly, just like that, after I had tried for MONTHS, he looked at me like he completely understood, and he walked away and that was it. My goddamn millet-growing sister was right. I had underestimated little Alfie, as well as big Colleen.

Weaning is hard, pumping is hard, it's all fucking hard. But great! But HARD. I have so much respect for women who go into an office and pump between meetings all day long. Since I work from home, and often from my bed with a newborn, I didn't have to sneak off to a coat closet or my car to pump and keep my boobs from getting engorged. I did get a pump based on recommendations from moms on social media that I have never met, because the mom army is strong and I trust them. Except for the ones who tell me things like use meat tenderizer on your nipples to get them ready for breastfeeding, as if I were a walking pot roast, or that nursing will rot my baby's teeth. It's breastmilk, not Mountain Dew! It's full of protein and vitamins and potassium—not brominated vegetable oil, whatever that is!

The *great* advice was amazing, though. I literally asked which pump was best and bought the one with the most likes in the comments. It was the Spectra, for anyone wondering. It's fucking awesome and one hundred dollars at Target (but insurance might cover it). It was so clutch when Alfie was a baby and I had to go to New York for a Facebook event, and I was sneaking away and pumping between Q&A sessions. By the way, this was the first time I was away from my baby and I was feeling that mix of separation anxiety and total bliss—like I could sleep in and café-hop, and then sleep again if I wanted to! It's kind of a mind-fuck, because one second you are missing your baby IN YOUR BONES, and the next you're like, hell yes, I am FREE! That paradox pretty much defines motherhood, though.

If breastfeeding has taught me anything, besides how to keep two tiny humans alive, it is that boobs are a hot topic. Obviously, since I felt the need to stuff toilet paper in my bra as a kid, I suspected they had power. But until I became an accidental lactivist, I had no idea just how much power, and milk, they held. I have a theory that I'm pretty sure is scientific, and it's that men who were breastfed are boob guys, and if they were formula-fed they're ass men. Stephen was formula-fed, and he's all about that ass. My friend Jack's husband, who was breastfed, loves big boobs, and he is gay. So you see how solid this theory is. It falls apart if you apply any logic to it whatsoever, but I believe in it. But most of all, I believe in boibs.

CHAPTER 4

Did I Marry a Narcissist?

If you are reading this book partly because you think Stephen and I are #relationshipgoals and you want to find out exactly how to have the perfect partnership, keep reading. Because what you believe to be true is only the beginning of our utterly faultless marriage. Fighting over our driving habits? NEVER. Arguing about how I clutter our bathroom vanity with over fifty different nearly empty bottles of oils, lotions, and serums? NOT A CHANCE. Do we brawl over who did the last diaper? Nope, because he actually loves to do them. The only thing better than our incredible communication skills is our athletic and sensuous sex life. He does whatever I desire and always with a tender smile. I get a bouquet of Juliet roses every morning and he gets . . . *me*. We can't even remember the last time we've disagreed, because we are more in sync than the iconic '90s boy band.

PLEASE TELL ME YOU KNOW I'M KIDDING.

One thing I'm noticing more and more is that THERE IS NO PERFECT RELATIONSHIP. To my knowledge, it just doesn't exist. I can't think of a couple I know that doesn't have issues in SOME way, shape, or form. And the couples who claim they have no issues? I CALL BULLSHIT! And I don't think this is a bad thing! It actually makes me feel much less alone to know that I cannot think of any couple who doesn't struggle with SOMETHING. Stephen and I have been *through* it. Several times. But we've always managed to get through the shitty bits, the bad days, the sometimes-I-want-to-strangle-you-even-though-I-fucking-love-you moments. And there have been a lot of those moments. On both sides.

After our daughter was born, we got into a fight so awful I found myself googling things like "Am I married to a narcissist?" But hey, you may ask, don't we all have *some* narcissistic traits? Maybe not the I-have-zero-empathy-and-might-just-ruin-your-life variety, but more like the sometimes-I-watch-my-own-Insta-stories-several-times-in-a-row type. Are narcissists like plants? Are there varietals? Do they come in thirty-one toxic flavors? Can we taste a rainbow of egomania? Can you Build-A-Bear your own unbearable asshole? You tell me! All I know is, we all have the potential to be jerks and it doesn't necessarily mean we are full-blown narcissists. I also don't ever want to trivialize the very real pain faced by victims of clinical narcissism. It's an overused and complicated word. I think the word is tossed around WAY too casually, especially by me while I too casually googled it in regard to my husband. Narcissism is a personality disorder, not an insult to hurl around the kitchen because he forgot to make me coffee.

So, because we are not perfect, my main response to the common question "How do you guys make it work?" would probably be: I don't fucking know!

Clearly, there is no such thing as a Brady Bunch family where the parents never fight and the biggest dilemmas are things like Jan trying to erase the freckles on her face with lemon juice (though a *very* tense and dramatic episode). My marriage is awesome overall (the couple who dances in adult diapers together stays together), but Stephen and I are terrible at fighting. We don't fight often, but when we do, it is not good. It is *Transformers*-meets-*King-Kong* levels of destruction, without the popcorn or cool special effects. (Fun fact: Stephen scored both of those films!) We have definitely had our serious issues, and we continue to work to heal, with the help of our AA sponsors and our psychiatrist. We also just naturally like each other, which helps. So, I don't have the secret, but I do have some stories.

When I researched characteristics of a narcissist so I could armchair diagnose my husband, he DID check off a few of the boxes. But then there were some more characteristics that he did not check, thank goodness. Still, this was during a time when I was so emotionally mixed up and having serious postpartum issues, so I actually felt sick to my stomach and started wondering whether or not I married a sociopathic monster. I vividly imagined that I'd have to take Alfie and Poppy and a suitcase full of snacks and go live back at my parents' house in Downers Grove. The movie in my head was horrendous.

The reason for our latest fight? It was not because someone cheated (more on that topic later) or because Stephen blew our life savings doing online gambling or buying rare vintage synthesizers from the 1970s. It was because we talked about work after eight o'clock at night.

We have this rule that we stop all work talk at a certain time every night so that we can just focus on other things, like each other, our kids, or what to watch on Netflix. The fact that we work together (at home), live together (also at home), and raise our kids together (with the help of our nanny Carla, at home) means that we need to turn it off at a certain point. We need to stop stressing about work and deadlines, otherwise we get into dumb arguments. We're so exhausted and we become two idiots who have no idea how to communicate. Maybe it's like a platypus trying to converse with a sloth? I'm assuming a lot, but I feel like sloths don't give a flying fuck. They're just like, "I'm 100 percent the cutest mammal on the planet and I know it." Also, according to some random article on the internet, sloths are incredible hosts to tiny animals like worms and beetles who burrow in their hair and eat scrumptious algae that grows there. Okay, sloths are disgusting and should be ashamed. And so should Stephen when I tell you what he did next!

So one night when Poppy was about six weeks old, Stephen broke our rule. And then, either because I wasn't eating my placenta or Stephen wasn't eating me or because sometimes marriage is hard, it all went to hell.

My mom had been staying with us for six weeks helping with the babies, which was wonderful and amazing and we could not have gotten through it without her, but . . . SIX WEEKS. So on this night my mom and I finished watching an Aretha Franklin docuseries at 10 p.m., and I was feeling 10 percent inspired by the Queen of Soul and 90 percent like a zombie who accidentally ate a bunch of melatonin, when Stephen strolled in and started talking about a brand deal that we needed to film the next day. I knew my mom felt left out when we started talking about deliverables and social media content, so I always tried to include her in the conversations—by repeating and explaining every single thing we just said. For those SIX WEEKS, our conversations went a little like this:

Stephen: Laura, we need to deliver the cut to Jason by nine in the morning . . .

Laura: Mom, "the cut" means our video, and Jason is my Facebook contact . . . Okay, Stephen, sounds—

Mom: TELL JASON HE HAS TO WAIT—YOU JUST HAD A BABY!

Or . . .

Stephen: Laura, we have a call tomorrow with Roger, and then one right after that with Jason to talk about the nipple cover . . .

Laura: Mom, Roger is our contractor for the new house, he's great, and Jason is our Facebook point person, remember? So I guess we talked about urine and spit-up too much in our recent video and if there are too many bodily functions, Facebook won't monetize a video and that's how we pay our mortgage . . .

Mom: I DON'T LIKE THIS JASON—YOU NEED ANOTHER FACEBOOK CONTRACTOR!

Laura: Mom, Jason isn't a contractor . . .

Mom: Well, I don't like him!

Laura: Okay, Mom, I'll just call Mark Zuckerberg and tell him I want the video that shows Poppy peeing in my face to be monetized!

Mom: I can't see why you wouldn't. It's natural AND THEY NEED YOU!

Stephen's frustration increased every time my mother chimed in with her well-meaning but misguided advice.

Stephen: Laura? We need to decide whether or not we are going to—

Mom: GODDAMMIT, NO! Just tell them her perineum is still sore and she can't film tomorrow!

Anyway, long story long—we broke our rule. Our *psychiatrist-prescribed* rule.

All three of us were overly tired and stressed, and we started spiraling in our own unique and shitty ways. My mom continued giving us unsolicited advice while watching us run in circles. Stephen and I were arguing about a brand deal like we were handling nuclear codes, when in reality it was for a PopSocket. When we argue, I usually want to hash the issue out then and there. I want us to be on the same team and try to figure it out in the moment, but Stephen needs time to process things. He needs to think, and while he thinks, I spiral even more and convince myself he's a serial killer. My mom was on my side (obviously), and what I know now is that Stephen felt ganged up on. He got completely silent, and then he just walked away. One of the narcissist's traits is disregard for other people's feelings, and in that moment my feelings felt tossed away, ghosted, and crushed to oblivion by a fifty-ton road roller. I am not exaggerating—that's exactly how it felt. What I didn't take into account was that as a child Stephen sometimes felt ganged up on by his mother and father, and this brought back deep unresolved trauma for him.

When we went to bed, we broke another basic rule of marriage: Never go to sleep angry. In the morning when I tried to talk to Stephen, he was still silent, and to me that's unacceptable. That behavior is so triggering for me. My therapist says it brings up memories of dysfunction in my house growing up, living with a dad who drank all the time and could have a very Jekyll-and-Hyde personality. The silent treatment makes me feel extremely insecure in relationships in general, and then when you bring kids into the picture, it's a million times worse. When you don't have kids you can say, "Screw you,

I'm out of here!" and you can pack your knapsack and leave for a couple of days. With kids, everything is so much more serious, and you can't just walk out when they physically need your tit. Arguments with Stephen, now that we have children, are much scarier for me. It's like my emotions are on steroids and my mind is on acid, minus anything about that which might sound fun.

I started freaking out that Stephen might one day give our kids the silent treatment, and then what if he just abandoned all three of us and took off to Morocco? And then what if he disappeared in Morocco and we never heard from him again until Alfie and Poppy were in their twenties and they went searching for him in the desert, and found him living in a cave with nothing but a keyboard and an endless stockpile of canned lentils? Instead of having all of these thoughts and feelings, like my life was completely out of control and my world was crumbling and my husband was plotting an escape to North Africa, I could have taken a deep breath and said to myself: *Stephen just needs a day to process the argument. Do your thing and he'll come around when he's ready. And no, he's not a narcissist bound for Morocco. That's ridiculous, Laura. He barely likes to leave the house. Go for a walk.*

What I did do instead was panic-text my therapist and my sponsor for guidance. I know I am not perfect and I can also act in extremely irrational ways at times, like saying to Stephen that I want to end my life when I know in reality I never would. That must cause him extreme insecurity and it's just never okay. I'm still working on impulse control. One of the most important things I was taught in early sobriety was to reach out to someone and figure out my part in the situation, no matter how small. They say in recovery that resentment is our number-one offender and it's the first thing that will take us out. So it is beyond important for us to right our wrongs and keep our side of the street clean whenever possible. For me, that means taking some responsibility, becoming willing to forgive, searching to find where I had gone wrong, and doing everything in my power to make it right. Even if this sounds like my ego's worst nightmare, it's essential for my recovery and serenity.

I headed out on my morning tranquility walk feeling anything but tranquil. I was desperately trying to sweat out the fear and anxiety I was feeling. And then, there she was . . . my guiding light . . . Saint Anne. Purposefully strolling up that hill with such agility and grace. I just KNEW she would have the answer. So I kindly accosted her for the fifth time. "God damn it, not that lanky blonde again," I heard her mumble under her breath. But I was desperate, so I approached her anyway. We exchanged pleasantries and then I immediately asked her for the secret to her nearly fifty-year relationship. She paused for a moment, musing over her response, because sages ALWAYS pause before they impart great wisdom during a Tuesday morning stroll.

"Well, we were in our forties when we met," Anne said. I was hanging on her every word. "He loved horses—over the years, we had over fifty horses—and I was very involved with medicine. There were times we would be sitting in a restaurant waiting to be served and I would get an emergency call and have to go to the hospital. He never once got upset with me or blamed me for ruining our dinner. He just respected it. He respected me. He respected my lifestyle, I respected his, and we coordinated."

She paused, looking into the distance like a seer, before adding, "I liked the man he WAS, not the man I was going to make him into."

DAMN THAT ANNE FOR ALWAYS SAYING THE PER-FECT THING.

I needed to respect the person Stephen was, and he needed to do the same for me. Anne and I parted ways, and she trudged off in her flowy linen pants, her pink sun hat, and her hand-to-God halo.

I cannot afford to hold on to my anger or treat people poorly. If I lose my sobriety, I lose everything. So I know how important it is to check myself and admit my own part in fights. Sometimes it's tough to get Stephen to understand just how I am feeling. So after a full day of dark, intrusive thoughts, I decided to communicate my feelings to my husband in the best, healthiest way I knew: I made a video about how depressed I was feeling. Remember the mental breakdown video I spoke about before where I opened up about my PPD? Well, this argument with Stephen was the thing that ulti-mately sparked it. I guess, part of me was hoping he would see it and understand how much pain I was feeling and just talk to me again.

I didn't initially intend to make that video, though. I desperately needed to get out of the house, alone, for a few minutes. My heart was breaking, as this was day two of Stephen ignoring me. It was so hurtful, I felt as though he'd stopped loving me. I was dealing with PPD and this was just the icing on the cake. I asked my mom to watch the kids while I drove to get a coffee. I sat in the parking lot and started bawling. I didn't have a napkin, so I grabbed a diaper and blew my nose in it. Then, I sort of chuckled. This was a low point, even for me. I thought, *I can't be alone in this. There must be other women blowing their noses in diapers, feeling like all is lost.* I decided to film it. The mind-fuck of being a vlogger is that whenever I'm experiencing something intense and personal, a tiny part of my brain goes, "Film this!" I could share a post where I'm saying, "Things are great, I'm so happy," and not many will care, but if I post something saying, "I'm not doing well, I feel depressed and my husband may be a narcissist," it will probably go viral.

I don't blame anyone for that. I think life is hard and people find it cathartic and refreshing when public figures have REAL conversations about what's REALLY going on. I'm certainly drawn to other people's dramas, conflict, and hardship. I want to know I'm not alone. Talking about conflict is so compelling because it's so relatable. It also connects us to each other and to our emotions and makes us feel better about our own lives. Consuming drama even causes me to secrete endorphins, which are weirdly pleasure-inducing. So yeah, being vulnerable and talking about my struggles has proven to be more popular than me vlogging about how great my matcha green tea latte tastes after yin yoga. One time, years ago when I was talking to my best friend Maggie, she was like, "Girl, I've got to go—I'm SO busy . . ." And then I quickly said, "Okay, good talking. By the way, I got dropped by my agent." She suddenly had all the time in the world to talk. "Wait, what? Tell me everything!! I need details." She's not a monster, but the horrible news lit up her brain circuits like a Vegas billboard. Who doesn't live for some good tea? Honestly!

Life is so much more interesting when we're honest about the hard shit. I love it when friends tell me that their husband or partner is being a jerk or their baby is being an asshole, because it makes me relate and feel connected. Does that make *me* a narcissist? Who knows? But one of the reasons I made that crying-in-the-car video was because I did not want to stay silent about what I was going through. I believe we are only as sick as our secrets. I also wanted Stephen to see what I was going through, and since he scores all our videos, I knew I'd have his undivided attention. Some might say it was disgusting of me to blow my nose in a newborn diaper on camera (CLEAN, OK?), but you know what I find more disgusting than that? Couples who pretend they're perfect all the time! Talk about ABOMINABLE.

After I filmed the video, I waited for Stephen to acknowledge my pain. My mom was Team Laura all the way (obviously). She kept telling me I did nothing wrong, which was making me feel like I should be even more upset and question the nature of my marriage—instead of just realizing that Stephen simply hadn't said *good morning* to me, which is rude but not divorce-worthy.

Lawyer: What were your irreconcilable differences?

Wife: On Monday, June 7, 2020, he didn't say *good morning*.

Lawyer: What else?

Wife: Oh, he wouldn't go on a walk with me because he needed time to think.

Lawyer: Fine, that'll be $63,700 for my time.

See? Not worth it!

The first time Stephen watched the video, he didn't say anything. *Still* not acknowledging my pain was another stab in the heart. You bet your ass I put another "x" on the Official Narcissist Checklist I'd created in my mind. I just wanted him to fucking see me! When the video finally posted, it opened up so many conversations with other women online about postpartum issues and relationships and mental health struggles. It helped me realize that the snotty diaper video was so much bigger and more disgusting than just me. It was a larger conversation, and I did feel seen. Not by my husband who was within line of sight, but by thousands of incredible women whom I did not even know.

That evening, I asked Stephen *again* if we could all go for a walk. He begrudgingly said yes, so I thought, *Finally we're getting somewhere*. He said he'd seen the video, but instead of feeling empathy, he was upset about the part where I cried out that I was angry at myself for not doing enough and my husband for not doing enough. The only thing he mentioned from this incredibly vulnerable and hard-to-make video about my mental struggles was that he was hurt that I didn't think *he* was doing enough. That was all he took from it, which hurt a lot. I told him that I just needed him to hug me and tell me everything was going to be okay. But he couldn't do that. He told me that he was also depressed. He was also in a terrible place and asked, how can I expect a broken person to fix another broken person? This was one of the moments where I wished I had married someone who was maybe neurotypical. Someone who was more stable, to offset me. Instead we are two neurodivergent recovering addicts who write songs about buttholes for a living—not exactly a recipe for the most emotional stability and rationality at all times.

Like I said, the good times are SO fucking good—so creative, so fulfilling, so passionate. But the bad times? Well . . . they're really bad. One of the things I struggle with the most is not letting someone else's bad mood affect mine. What a challenge that is! Thankfully, Stephen came into the bedroom that evening, letting me know that he had watched the video a second time. He looked at me with compassionate eyes, hugged me, and said, "I love you, I'm so sorry. I'm sorry you're struggling. I'm so sorry." I saw that he meant it. He was so far from narcissistic in that moment that I unchecked two of the boxes in my head. We then set up a call with our therapist, who reminded us to *"be curious, not furious."* Easier said than done, but super simple to remember because it rhymes!

Long before kids, we had some early blowouts (not the diaper kind). When we met, I was fifty-nine days sober. I know this because addicts count days like their life depends on it (because it does) and Stephen had 2,545 and a half days clean. Seven years. They say you don't get your marbles back until about five years into sobriety, and unfortunately in my case that is not an exaggeration. When we met, his marbles were pretty intact and mine were in total disarray. I was very antisocial and terrified of leaving the house because I was scared of relapsing. My sister had to literally FORCE me to go to the party where I ended up meeting Stephen. Nearly every day since I was about fifteen years old, I'd been drinking or using—and I was twenty-four years old when we met. My brain wasn't fully repaired and I was still early in working the Twelve Steps. Then, about three months into my sobriety, I relapsed. He told me that he couldn't be with me if I wasn't sober, and I knew he was telling the truth. I also knew I had to put my sobriety before our relationship, before my work, before anything else. They say "anything you put before your sobriety, you lose." I nearly lost Stephen, because he was dead serious about not being with me. I started working the steps again and we got back on track. That is, until the evil German "hacker" came into our lives . . .

Pretty early on when Stephen and I were dating, I met this woman I'll call Sylvia at an AA meeting. She had a very troubled childhood, to the point that her mom got her and her sister into escorting, and her dad was a full-blown coke addict. It was a sad story, and she was a beautiful woman with tons of totally understandable issues. Anyway, she asked me to sponsor her, so we started meeting regularly. One day at lunch she told me that she had a major sex and love addiction. Sadly, I still don't think enough people understand that sex addiction isn't some illicit thing that makes someone a creep. There's such a stigma around it, yet up to 30 million people (that we know of) in the U.S. are currently living with a sex addition. I think there's even more shame and stigma attached to sex addiction than to any other kind. Sex addicts get their hit through sex/flirting/love the same way drug addicts get their hit through dope. One day at lunch, Sylvia was telling me about the twenty guys she was having sex with, and when I said, "You have to be careful, you could get HIV," she replied, "I don't care." I'll never forget that. I'll also never forget that Sylvia spoke in a low monotone voice like Daria from the animated MTV show, and she punctuated every thought with, "WTF, I'm gonna puke . . ." So, for example, when I told her my big news that I was in love with a man who I thought might be "the one," she replied in a dull, dreary tone:

"WTF, I'm gonna puke . . ." But she meant it in the most loving way possible, I swear.

So that day at lunch, when she was monotoning about her twenty boyfriends who didn't know about one another, she dryly told me that she'd discovered a camera under boyfriend #6's computer desk . . . and that camera was, and I quote, at "dick level." She was absolutely convinced he was using it to get the perfect dick pic and she was probably right. She then discovered boyfriend #12 had been texting his ex. I had not been shocked that Sylvia had twenty secret boyfriends, but I WAS shocked that she had snooped through someone's phone.

"You've never checked Stephen's phone?" she droned.

"No, I've never snooped."

"WTF, I'm gonna puke," she said, actually putting some inflection in her tone, which made me very uneasy. "Laura, you *never* really know what's going on with guys, trust me. You think you know someone, but guys are *always* cheating and having affairs. *Always.* You have no idea the number of married men I've slept with."

It was my turn to say, "WTF? I'm gonna puke . . ."

That conversation really stuck with me. I knew she was (justifiably) crazy and trauma-dumping her own fucked-up experiences onto me, but it still stuck. Later on when we were in Stephen's Santa Monica apartment, I told him I'd had lunch with Sylvia.

"She was telling me that she snoops through her boyfriends'— plural—stuff, isn't that crazy?"

"Yeah, it really is crazy," he agreed. "You know, you can always look through my stuff, though. I don't care."

Then he went off to work scoring the latest *Transformers* movie with Hans Zimmer. There I was, pretty newly sober again, uninspired and unemployed, sitting all alone in his apartment with Sylvia's doom-and-gloom prophecy droning in my ears . . .

"You think you know someone, Laura . . ."

That was quickly followed by Stephen's words ringing in my mind:

"You can always look through my stuff. I don't care . . ."

. . . And so I did.

I took him up on his offer. I started looking at his emails. After all, he TOLD ME TO. Right?

At first it felt incredibly invasive, and I actually got shaky. I was in love with him and didn't know what I was doing, but I just couldn't stop myself. I didn't see anything in the emails other than 388 unread offers from Groupon, which I was tempted to clean up, *but then he would know*. I felt guilty and sick with shame. Then I realized that I could look at his Facebook messages! So I did that too.

After a few minutes of scrolling, I was about to stop and repent for my sins when all of a sudden there was a message from an attractive woman from Germany. So I clicked. The messages were very flirtatious, sexual, and . . . *recent*. The blood drained out of my body (maybe metaphorically, but MAYBE NOT). I felt like I might pass out. I couldn't believe what I was reading. She wanted to be a singer and loved that he produced music (WTF, I'm gonna puke), and she loved that he was handsome. Then HE wrote back saying that SHE was beautiful. I was devastated. Stephen was my Prince Charming. Our chemistry was off the charts, and before that moment I was totally convinced that he had ZERO flaws. He could do no wrong. Until now!

So, I did what any idiot in love would do. I projected his flirtatious conversation with the German whore onto his seventy-inch TV screen. While he was out scoring a mega-budget *Transformers* movie, I was ALSO working hard, transforming his living room into an interrogation theater. I wrangled wires and plugged cords into ports until stuff worked. I tested lighting setups and rearranged chairs for maximum effect. I did a sound check, even though her messages had no sound. And then like a psycho I sat there in the dark, with dramatic low lighting angled to create dim hues and mysterious shadows. Then I put on the soundtrack from *Vertigo* and waited for him to come home.

When he finally arrived, the drama began. I immediately lost my shit on him, to the point where he might have thought he'd entered into a *Fatal Attraction*–type situation. I pointed to the conversation projected on the massive TV and roared, "What the fuck is this?! Who the fuck is she? How the fuck could you! You fucking fuckface!" Insert any other psychotic dialogue here, because chances are

I screamed it. I may have even yelled, "Get me a bunny to boil!" And that's extra-alarming coming from a vegan.

He looked at the TV with his horrifically flirtatious conversation blown up on the big screen and said, without hesitation:

"Oh my God . . . that's disgusting!! Whoever wrote that is absolutely disgusting!"

Um, excuse me?

He pathetically doubled down:

"A hacker must have gotten into my computer and written those messages—I would NEVER! That is sick! That is really just plain sick."

A fucking HACKER? Was it Anonymous?! The Chaos Computer Club?! Neo and Trinity?! My brain hadn't fully recovered from the drugs yet, but I wasn't *completely* oblivious. I packed all my things, while weeping and yelling *Exorcist*-level blasphemies at him. I sounded like I eventually would during unmedicated childbirth— except instead of pushing a baby out of my coot, I was pushing Stephen out of my life. *And* my coot. NO COOT FOR YOU! I told him he was never, ever going to see me or my self-respecting coot ever again!

After only two short months together, we broke up. Around the same time, I had gotten into stand-up comedy and had my first big showcase at The Comedy Store, which was a huge deal for me. Stephen is *obsessed* with comedy, but I wouldn't let him come. He was heartbroken (GOOD!). This went on for a while, with him trying to get me back and me saying "fuck off." Stephen was extremely persistent, sending flowers, calling, and texting. He could be very charming. All he had to do was open his stupid funny British mouth, and certain women (like myself) swooned. He even offered to go to couples therapy with me. He said he would do anything to prove he loved me, so I said *fine*. I loved him, plus he wasn't just talking. He was willing to *do something*. I found it very attractive that he wanted to get into the solution, which is something that probably would have made Sylvia want to puke.

Stephen and I have had about four therapists over our ten-year relationship. There was one I'll call Deborah, who was always Xanaxed off her tits. She would start sessions in a whispery slur, "So . . . what's going on today guythhhh?" Once I explained the snooping and the German "hacker," she slurred, "Oh that's te*rrr-rrrr*ible. By the way, the man next door is a psychiatrist and if you feel anxious, he could really help you out. Like, *really* help you out. Like, a lot." Then she started snoring.

So eventually I went to see Deborah's psychiatrist-next-door, and within twenty minutes of meeting him he told me that I had anxiety and bipolar disorder and I should start lithium immediately.

"I don't believe I am bipolar. And I actually prefer yoga and meditation for anxiety," I said.

He leaned in and said, "I can make you feel like you just got out of a yoga class twenty-four hours a day." THIS IS A DIRECT QUOTE. FROM A DOCTOR. TO A RECOVERING DRUG ADDICT.

I was appalled by this guy's hubris and his misdiagnosis and his overall sleaziness. Talking to him helped me see why Deborah didn't help us as a couple AT ALL—she was tripping balls! Treed! Trollied! Blasted! Blitzed! Zooted off her tits! She had no idea what we were saying half the time. So we found another therapist. I could see Stephen's willingness to go to any lengths to change and address not just our issues but his possible sex and love addiction. The next woman we saw, Claire, was very young and just out of grad school. She was so nervous during the sessions that I'm pretty sure we were her first patients ever. I'm not a fan of passive therapy, where the counselor nods and says, "Uh-huh" and "interesting" and then "time's up!" Like, give me an assignment or some practical solutions or a handout to read. I WANT SOLUTIONS. I hated school as a kid, but as an adult, I wanted some knowledge!

That's one reason I love AA. Whenever I would call my sponsor and start ranting my problems at her, she would immediately cut me off: "Stop right there—I am not a therapist. Stop dumping your problems onto me. Go write down your resentment, make a personal inventory on it, and then call me back immediately to discuss. Now!" It sounds harsh, but I needed that. She forced me to get to the root cause of my problems—to keep the focus on me and what I can change. She taught me to find my part in any and all shitty situations. Where had I been selfish, self-seeking, dishonest, or afraid? Writing it all out forced me to dig deep and get into the solution, to become willing to forgive, and to keep my side of the street clean. THIS was freeing. Incessantly ranting about my problems all day and playing victim is FUN, but not productive. I needed to take action toward resolving my resentment. It is the only way for me.

At the end of the day, seeing that flirtatious DM was not worth my serenity. And let me be clear, it doesn't make what HE did right. Not at all. But me replaying his mistakes in my head did nothing for me. And so I say, God, grant me the serenity to accept the things I cannot change (what happened), have the courage to change the things I can (leave him or forgive him), and the wisdom to know the difference. Either I trust my higher power and surrender, or I play God (a.k.a. run the show and attempt to control everything).

Although, he DID say himself that I could look through his stuff whenever I wanted . . . so, maybe on some level he wanted me to find it?

Since we were not getting suggestions from Claire or learning trust-building exercises, we didn't stay with her for long. That's the thing about couples therapy—we needed to try out a few Deborahs, Claires, and drug-pushers before we found our match. I found the psychiatrist we see now via my good friend . . . Miley Cyrus.

Okay, I have actually never met Miley Cyrus, nor have I been anywhere remotely near her. I heard her talking to this doctor on an Instagram Live, and she swore by him. And when one thinks of Miley Cyrus, the first thought is mental stability. Right? Right??! Whatever, I liked what he had to say. He's funny and brilliant and he's always plugging his fucking books, but he does give great solutions and homework. So much homework.

Also, being willing to forgive someone doesn't mean you have to be a doormat or stay if that person is abusive or continues to make the same mistakes. After some time went by and we made it through our assembly line of therapists, I was able to forgive Stephen. I believed he was sorry. It was embarrassing for him to have to talk about the hacker thing, and I'm pretty sure that even Deborah held back some laughter through the Xanax. When I told my friend Sylvia about it, to my surprise, she didn't say, "WTF, I'm gonna puke."

She said, "WTF, I told you so."

If you are STILL not convinced that Stephen and I have issues, I can help! There is more. So much more.

A few months after the German hacker debacle, Stephen went to London to work on a movie score. We had gotten to a solid place again and he'd asked me to move in with him. I said not unless we were engaged, which really wasn't an ultimatum or some attempt to be a saint—I just *really* hate moving. If we weren't going to be together forever, I was not about to pack up my every possession. I had learned from my mistakes with Damon . . . and Rudolf . . . and Jake . . . Anyway, shortly after that he actually did propose, and so I moved in. We had been together for six months at this point. Anyway, I remember that I started to really miss him, like to an unhealthy degree. I became somewhat paranoid that while he was gone he was going to unexpectedly fall in love with a stunning British woman with a more sophisticated vocabulary and fashion sense than I had. My mind started playing tricks on me. I couldn't take being alone. I was absolutely codependent and somewhat addicted to Stephen. Because he wasn't there and I was all alone in his apartment, it felt like a good idea to pick up and numb out. I found my old dealer through social media and picked up my horrific drug of choice: cocaine. I proceeded to get high and drunk by myself in our apartment. It was four in the morning, I was high out of my mind, paranoid and obsessing about Stephen, when Sylvia's stupid monotone voice started droning in my ears again . . .

"Laura, you never really know what's going on . . . All men cheat."

So I decided to check Stephen's email. I couldn't help myself! I mean I *could*, but it was right there in front of me. At least, with a few clicks and some premeditated snooping it would be.

I looked at his most recent emails from that day and found one from a female executive at his record label. In it, she wrote that she had a dream about him (WTF! I'M GONNA PUKE!) and he said, "Oh, that's crazy. See you at the studio." And then . . . that was it. So of course, my coked-up, paranoid brain was like, "They are definitely, 100 percent in love and are going to start a life out there together and she is already definitely pregnant with his child." I lost my freaking shit. I was still traumatized by the German, had relapsed once again, and so decided to take matters into my own coked-out, codependent hands. I HAD to find out what was going on. I HAD to get to the bottom of it. "You were in my dream last night"?!! COME ON! There HAD to be SOMETHING going on. I was a proud, strong, strung-out woman who needed answers!!! So . . . I emailed this woman back . . . FROM STEPHEN'S EMAIL . . . AS IF I WERE STEPHEN.

I wrote (please brace yourself):

"Did we have sex last night? I can't remember."

Then I hit SEND.

DID WE HAVE SEX LAST NIGHT? *I CAN'T REMEMBER.*

The next day, I got a frantic call from Stephen. I picked up, casually, as if I HAD DONE NOTHING WRONG.

"Hi, babe."

"Laura, are you fucking kidding me?"

He was livid.

"Are you out of your fucking mind?!!"

Not only was I hungover and full of shame from my relapse, I was humiliated about what I had done. At first I tried to pretend I didn't know what he was talking about.

"What, babe? How's London? Are you near that massive clock? Big Ben? Make sure to take some photos . . ."

He paused. The silence was deafening. Then he yelled:

"Did we have sex last night . . . I CAN'T REMEMBER?!!!!"

"Huh? Oh . . . that . . . must have been . . . a hacker."

"LAURA!!!"

"Okay. Okay. Yeah . . . That was me. Sorry about that. But why is she emailing you about seeing you in her dreams?! Don't you think that's a little inappropriate???!"

"I CAN'T CONTROL HER DREAMS, LAURA! BUT SHE CAN CONTROL WHETHER I HAVE A FUCKING JOB! SHE'S THE HEAD OF THE FUCKING RECORD LABEL! ARE YOU FUCKING KIDDING ME?! YOU'RE COMPLETELY INSANE."

"A little bit, yes," I admitted. "But more importantly . . . did you have sex with her, I can't remember?!"

"No!!!!! Christ on a bike, NO!!!!"

"Okay, great, I'll see you soon, babe!"

I hung up quickly, before he could tell me to cancel my flight.

Before all of this, Stephen had booked a ticket for me to visit him during the second half of his trip to London, and I still went. I remember arriving at the fancy five-star hotel in Soho and meeting him at the café. He was already sitting at the table as I walked up. I sat down, he looked at me for a couple of seconds, and he immediately said, "You relapsed, didn't you?"

I paused, contemplating lying to him. But I couldn't. He just KNEW. So I came clean about not being clean.

"Yes, I did. I was scared. I was paranoid. I was insecure. I hated that you were gone. I'm sorry. It's not going to happen again. I want sobriety. I want you."

I thought it was going to be over, as this wasn't the first time I had slipped in our six months together. Instead, he looked at me with deep empathy. He really understood my struggle in such a deeply profound way. He was also madly in love with me and extremely pussy-whipped. He didn't want to lose me either . . . even though I was acting BATSHIT CRAZY. Even though I could have gotten him fired from his job. Even though I had relapsed once again. He forgave me, and we actually ended up having an incredible trip. It felt like a new beginning. And that record executive? Well, I never met her. I stayed back at the hotel while he went to the studio. I was NOT about to show my face there. Fuck, I'm an *idiot*. I'm sure he was mortified that he had to explain to this executive that his recovering fiancée was INCREDIBLY unhinged, but we somehow made it through that horrible ordeal too.

Still not convinced that Stephen and I don't have it ALL figured out?! Do you need more evidence? Not a problem.

Before I wow you with Exhibits X, Y, and Z, a quick sidenote. I know our relationship sounds utterly fucked since I'm telling you all our worst moments, back-to-back. These were some of the stories I was too scared to tell in my first book for fear of judgment, but what I'm starting to learn is that vulnerability is strength (thanks, Brené Brown). And I'm most likely not alone here. It's just that no one seems to talk about this shit. *I* didn't even want to talk about this shit. But things have changed since my first book, so get ready. Okay, here we go. I'm going . . . Brace yourself! Now I'll begin . . . I'm not stalling, *you're* stalling. Fine, grab some fucking popcorn; here's the hardest story I've ever had to tell. It happened eight years ago, and it's still tough to talk about:

A couple years into our relationship, Stephen got into a sort-of bad car accident. Okay, I think it was a light fender-bender, but *apparently* he had some back pain after it. He went to the doctor and quickly found out that in America, doctors will casually hand out highly addictive pain medications despite the widespread devastation caused by America's opioid epidemic. Any doctor who knowingly prescribes addictive pills to an *addict* should be strung up by their eyeballs AND their balls, if they have them (I'm not usually violent, but in this case I am). Anyway, he started losing weight and acting a bit strange. He would go on bike rides at four in the morning and come back all bruised because "Piss and tits, I fell off me old bike again. Didn't see the little tree there." I would hear pills rattling around in the bathroom, and when I asked about them he said he needed them and they were doctor prescribed. I asked him exactly what he was taking. He told me he had issues with anxiety, so he was prescribed Xanax. Issues with back pain from the accident, so Vicodin and Oxy. And issues with sleep, so Ambien.

I was outraged that doctors were prescribing this deadly concoction of incredibly powerful pills to an openly recovering addict. And I was furious with Stephen for taking them, but there was no getting through to him. He was sticking by his story that he was "still sober" because these were "doctor prescribed" and he "needed" them. He even went so far as to celebrate his AA sobriety birthday while high on pills. They call that "taking a dirty cake." Which sounds vile and is. It was a scary four or five months. I felt truly powerless. I still loved him so much, even though his behavior was becoming increasingly erratic. One morning, I was having a sleep-in (major pre-kids perk), and he was writing in his home studio in the next room. Eventually I woke up to a cell phone alarm going off. I checked my phone, and it wasn't *my* alarm. I tried to sleep through the loud BEEP BEEP BEEP, but it just kept going off. It sounded like it was coming from the kitchen. If it wasn't my phone, it must have been Stephen's. I yelled from bed, half-asleep, for Stephen to turn it the fuck off. He couldn't hear me because his studio door was shut. He was playing music, loudly, and definitely zooted on pills. Still, I yelled again. "STEPHEN! TURN YOUR ALARM OFF! IT'S ONLY TEN FORTY-FIVE IN THE MORNING!"

Still nothing. The incessant beeping continued. I think it actually got LOUDER, or at least it seemed to.

I angrily pushed the warm covers off my still-drowsy body and stormed into the kitchen to turn off his phone. Within a split second, my world began to crumble. The very moment I grabbed his phone to turn it off, a message popped up.

"Are we still meeting this morning?"

At first I didn't think anything of it, partly because I was still half-asleep. But then, I noticed that the contact name was *"Absolutely No Way."*

Huh, I thought as my brain started to jolt awake. *That's strange. Someone named "Absolutely No Way" wants to know if they are going to meet this morning.* I was genuinely confused. Then, I opened the text thread . . . and my whole universe shattered.

I saw texts like, *"Did you like the trousers I was wearing the other day? Were they sexy?"* and *"Remember on the kitchen counter?* ☺ *"*

My hands were shaking. My face went whiter than it already was. I still to this day have no clue where my blood went, because it sure as hell left my body. My heartbeat doubled in speed and I felt sick to my stomach, dizzy. Because I felt like my bones had just melted away, I leaned against the kitchen counter—hopefully not the same one referred to in the text. I was so incredibly shocked, devastated, and heartbroken. Looking back, I don't know how I could have been so blindsided. Not only had he struggled with love addiction in the past, he was OFF HIS NUTS on four different hard-core prescription drugs. He was NOT himself. Still, I'm not excusing him, and meanwhile I was crushed.

Stephen remained in his studio, completely oblivious to the fact that his alarm had been going off for the last thirty minutes and that his WIFE had picked it up and discovered his MISTRESS. He was high in his little studio, vibing and blissfully unaware that he was about to be justifiably murdered.

My breathing was fast and my racing mind was faster. I knew that if I confronted him at that moment, when he was in the state he was in, he would get defensive and give me some bullshit excuse about the whole thing. Active addicts are notorious liars. I know this because I was one. I KNEW I wouldn't get anywhere by confronting him right then, and I needed answers. So I ran to the bathroom with his phone, locked the door, and replied to the text as Stephen:

Yeah, I'll meet you, what's the address again?

Pretty clever, right?

This bitch *thought* she was going to meet Stephen, but showing up instead would be my lanky ass that doesn't know how to fight and was once beaten up in high school by a girl who was four foot eleven.

Still shaking, I stared at the phone with tears in my eyes, desperately waiting for a response. Then I saw the three dots indicating that she was typing a reply. My eyes got even wider than they already were: She sent the address.

Huh. I knew exactly where it was. It was an AA meeting in the Pacific Palisades, one of the biggest meetings in Los Angeles. Hundreds of people would attend this weekend. So he was having an affair with someone in the program? WOW. That really stung. This was supposed to be a place where people became BETTER. Where we practice rigorous honesty, where we continually work to keep our side of the street clean. But there was nothing clean about this. I needed to go. I needed to find her. I wasn't thinking straight. I was in fight-or-flight mode. I needed answers and I knew I wouldn't get them from him. I needed to know who was this person who destroyed our (sort of) beautiful marriage. Now, of course, I understand that person was in the next room, out of his mind on OxyContin . . .

I hid his phone in my purse, and fake-calmly knocked on his studio door.

"Come in," he said.

"Hey, babe. I'm going to run out quickly for a coffee. Do you need anything?"

Unlike the German hacker situation, *this* was not snooping. It was not me "trying to run the show" or "control" anyone. I firmly believe it was my higher power, showing me exactly what I needed to see in that moment. My higher power was *literally sounding an alarm.* I tried to ignore the alarm and pretend it wasn't happening (like I had been doing in our relationship). But it JUST. KEPT. GOING. OFF! I called for him to turn it off. He wasn't listening. The alarm rang louder. LAURA, WAKE UP. LAURA, WAKE UP! my higher power insisted through each piercing beep. LAURA, YOU NEED TO SEE WHAT IS HAPPENING. YOU NEED TO FUCKING WAKE UP. BEEP. BEEP. FUCKING BEEP. It took every ounce of energy and courage I had to pretend that everything was fine. I was holding back tears (and throat punches), but I just could not let on. Not yet.

Oblivious, he slurred, "Nope. I'm good. Just writing this piece for *Mission Impossible*. I may be going to an AA meeting in a bit," he said sheepishly.

THE FUCKING AUDACITY. YOU FUCKING PIG, I thought.

"Oh!" I responded sweetly. I was about to make *his* mission impossible. "Maybe I should go with you! We can go together!"

What's he gonna do now?! What's the fucking plan, Casanova?!

I was fascinated to see how he was going to get out of this one.

"Well, I'm super busy with work, actually. I don't think I'm going to go."

"Right," I said, doing my best to pretend to sound normal. Obviously, I knew he was lying to cover up and it fucking killed me inside.

We looked at each other for a moment. He looked almost dead inside. Frankly, so did I. And then I left, with his phone in my purse.

I sped down the Pacific Coast Highway heading into Malibu. The majestic blue ocean and glittering California sun were like insults to how I was actually feeling: devastated, vengeful, and totally beyond recall.

And then . . . Stephen's phone got another text.

ABSOLUTELY NO WAY: You almost here?

STEPHEN (ACTUALLY LAURA): Yup, see you soon!

I kept driving south along the ocean, trying to keep my hands from shaking. I had no clue what I was going to do if I saw "Absolutely No Way." How would I even know who she was? Did she know I existed? Would she recognize me and run? Would I chase her with a folding chair?

While I was driving I got an email from Stephen, asking if I had accidentally taken his phone. I couldn't hold it in any longer and I emailed him back, which is incredibly reckless:

Did I accidentally take your phone, you ask? ABSOLUTELY
NO WAY

(Clever, right?)

He started manically emailing me things like, "What? What are you talking about? Where are you? What are you doing?!"

After that, I ignored his emails. I was only a few minutes from the building when his "find my iPhone" went off. He was tracking me. I was on a mission, though, driven totally by emotion, and nothing was going to stop me. I pulled up to the giant AA meeting, parked, took a massive deep breath, and walked into a room packed with about three hundred people. I was dizzy with rage. The overwhelming stench of stale cigarette smoke and weak coffee intensified my nausea even more. I scanned the room for anyone who looked even mildly guilty, which, let's be real, was a large percentage of the room.

People were talking and having their coffee and acting like it was just another day, but for me the world was spinning. I felt like my feet were barely touching the ground. The voices and colors blurred together. I tried to zero in on the faces, to find THE face. I then called Absolutely No Way's phone while intensely scouring the room looking for a homewrecker to pick up the call . . . but she wasn't picking up. There was no answer. Also, there were a lot of people on their phones. Would she be a petite blonde? A redhead with glasses? A tall brunette? I spun around the room LOOKING for a girl who would be LOOKING back at me. But everyone was looking at me, because I looked crazy and possibly not sober. My breathing was rapid, my heart was pounding . . . Some tatted-up guy with a collared shirt offered me a newcomer chip and I told him to fuck off. I was on a mission and I needed no distractions. I was ready for the moment that I'd land on the right person and just know . . .

But I never found her. How could I? There were three hundred people to choose from. Eventually, my breath began to slow a bit, and I had a brief moment of clarity. WHAT WAS I DOING? WHY WAS I HERE? WHY wasn't I at home confronting my own husband about his affair? WHY had I sped to the Palisades to find HER? SHE was not to blame. HE was my problem, NOT her. And really, what

Newborn Laura. SO much hair.
Courtesy of the Clery family

My first-ever photo. My uncle Don bought me hair mousse as a christening present.
Courtesy of the Clery family

Little baby Stephen and his parents.
Courtesy of the Hilton family

My mom and dad circa 1974. They were twenty-two and twenty-three years old.
Courtesy of the Clery family

Daddy and me.
Courtesy of the Clery family

My mom gave me a Hawaiian-themed birthday, including a homemade hula girl cake.
Courtesy of the Clery family

I cut my own hair.
Courtesy of the Clery family

My dad, always without fail, stood behind my mother to make us laugh for the photo. Every year.
Courtesy of the Clery family

My sisters and me moments after playing in the rain.
Courtesy of the Clery family

Splits on the net-less trampoline. A core memory.
Courtesy of the Clery family

As a ten-year-old, plotting the theme for
my next horror musical.
Courtesy of the Clery family

Why were underwater pics EVERYTHING in the '90s?
Courtesy of the Clery family

Maggie and I, desperate for womanly curves,
used to cut out our tiny children heads and
glue them onto Victoria's Secret model bodies.
We really thought no one would notice.
Courtesy of the Clery family

My grandmother Alice at sixteen in 1939, high
school graduation at an all-girls Catholic school.
She looks much more serious than I was.

Courtesy of the Clery family

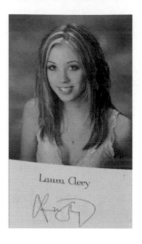

High school senior photo. Where
are my brows?

Courtesy of the author

At least I won something . . .

Courtesy of the author

Me, high in high school. WTF EYEBROWS.

Courtesy of the Clery family

With my beautiful cousin
on Christmas Eve.

Courtesy of the Clery family

My beautiful mama opening what were most definitely slippers or a robe.
Courtesy of the Clery family

Still cuddle with my mama today.
Courtesy of the Clery family

As a twenty-year-old starving actress.
Courtesy of the author

Nineteen and trying to fit the mold.
Photograph by Karin Catt

At twenty-two, high on cocaine, all skin and bones.
Courtesy of the author

On the set of yet another
failed pilot where I played
a dumb model.
Courtesy of the author

On set playing an emotionally unstable actress
(not sure why they cast me).
Courtesy of the author

Stephen and I had just started falling in love, circa
2011. My best friend Jack ruined the photo.
Courtesy of the author

My sister and I, young, naive, and
navigating Los Angeles.
Courtesy of Jackie Sobiszewski

We eloped just the two of us
and all we have to show for it
is a screenshot from a Vimeo
montage. Who loses all their
wedding photos? WE DO!
Courtesy of the author

Stephen during his relapse.
Courtesy of the author

At the guesthouse I rented when
Stephen and I separated
Courtesy of the author

We are both equally insane.
Photograph by David Cash

In 2016, when Helen
Horbath was born.
Courtesy of the author

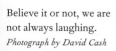

Believe it or not, we are
not always laughing.
Photograph by David Cash

Alfie's birth, April 20, 2019. I still couldn't feel
my legs, hence the smile.

Courtesy of the author

Newborn Alfie, straight-up cuddling with
Stephen.

Courtesy of the author

Le Pain Quotidien. This was when I got the hate
comment telling me to "put my BOIBS away."

Courtesy of the author

Our first-ever Boibs photo shoot.

Photograph by Chris Breitinger

Pregnant with Poppy. Is bloated an emotion?
Because it should be.
Photograph by Karin Catt

Me trying to look elegant and not piss myself.
Photograph by Karin Catt

Me trying to be Beyoncé . . .
Photograph by Karin Catt

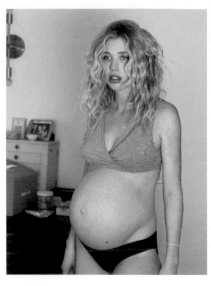

The day before I went into labor with Poppy.
Courtesy of the author

Laboring at home.
Courtesy of the author

Poppy's birth . . . shoot me.
Courtesy of the author

Poppy's birth, in transition. Stephen was so incredibly supportive here.
Courtesy of the author

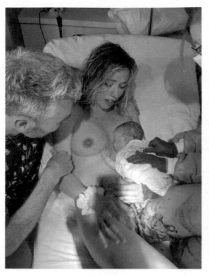

SHE'S OUT! WE DID IT!
Courtesy of the author

I was desperate for the pain to stop. I just wanted to marvel at my baby.
Courtesy of the author

Icing my coot while making uncontrollable, high-pitched moans. FUN!
Courtesy of the author

With Poppy.
Courtesy of the author

The day we got back from the hospital. Alfie finally met Poppy.

Courtesy of the author

The joys of motherhood.

Courtesy of the author

My thirty-fifth birthday. Also, Alfie in his regression.

Courtesy of the author

THIS IS POSTPARTUM.

Courtesy of the author

Poppy's smile solves all problems.
Courtesy of the author

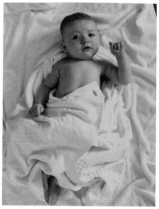

Little Alfie looking like a model.
Courtesy of the author

Stunningly beautiful baby Poppy.
Courtesy of the author

Little Laura.
Courtesy of the Clery family

Cheeky Alfie.
Courtesy of the author

Poppy fell asleep 90 percent of
the time in her sink baths.
Courtesy of the author

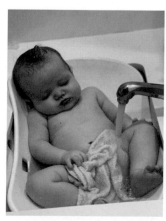

Sleepyhead in the bath.
Courtesy of the author

We need a bigger bath.

Courtesy of the author

Coming out of my postpartum depression.

Courtesy of the author

My ninety-eight-year-old hero, Anne.

Courtesy of the author

Always been a clown.

Robert Trachtenberg / Trunk Archive

My mother and Alfie.

Courtesy of the author

Seeing things from his perspective.

Courtesy of the author

Shortly after Alfie started speech therapy and was making amazing progress.

Courtesy of the author

Working mom.

Courtesy of the author

Neurodivergent family.
Photograph by Karin Catt

Alfie has such a lovely smile here.
Photograph by Karin Catt

did I think would have happened had I found her? I probably would have just gotten my gangly ass beaten up yet again. I walked out of that building defeated and drained, and I drove home.

I got back to the apartment, hurried straight into the bathroom, and locked myself in. I had a powerful feeling that Stephen would not tell me the truth and I had to find out what happened. Asking Absolutely No Way was my only shot at finding out the truth. I remember sitting on the toilet seat, frantically typing Absolutely No Way's number into my phone so I could reach out to her for answers. As I saved the number, I gasped, "WHAT THE FUCK . . . I'M GONNA PUKE."

The number was already in my phone as "Heidi AA."

I realized I must know this woman.

HEIDI AA? WHO THE FUCK IS HEIDI AA?!

A huge part of AA is exchanging numbers with other women so you can be of service to them whenever they need you. It's one alcoholic helping another. Or in this case, one alcoholic helping herself to another alcoholic's alcoholic husband. My phone was FULL of numbers with identifiers like "Sarah AA" or "Melanie AA" or "Con Artist Carly AA." I never added last names, just "AA," because *anonymous*. I had no recollection of who Heidi was. At least, not at first.

I quickly scanned my already short-circuiting brain to figure out which woman this could be. Was it the ex–heroin addict who owned a chain of strip clubs? No, that was Hilda AA. Was it the recovering cokehead who worked at Ben & Jerry's? No, that was Hilary AA. The former child star who kicked pills and then moved to Dubai? No, that was Lindsay AA. And then . . .

I just *knew*.

My mind vividly flashed back to HEIDI. A pretty woman with short black hair, both her arms entirely covered in tattoos. She was the opposite of me aesthetically, which somehow made it all even worse. Heidi was the one who I occasionally caught staring at me in meetings. Yes, it was her. I remembered her distinctly now. She had come up to me one day after I shared my story at a meeting. She sweetly said, "I really love your story and your sobriety. Can we exchange numbers?" They always say in AA to reach out to the people who "have what you want." I'm not sure someone's *husband* is what they mean, though. We exchanged numbers and that was that. I would occasionally notice her looking at Stephen and me at meetings, but I never thought much of it.

As soon as I opened the bathroom door, there he was, looking like a stoned pug with his tail between his legs. I shook my head in disgust and started to walk out the door. He followed.

"WAIT!" he cried out, looking absolutely petrified.

I looked into his bloodshot eyes. "I'm done waiting for you, Stephen. I'm done."

I walked out the front door. He followed.

"It was nothing! She is nothing!"

We were now standing outside our front door. "HOW COULD YOU DO THIS TO ME?! TO US?! FUCK YOU! IT'S OVER!"

And then I smacked him across the face . . . as HARD as my twiggy self could. In shock, he asked for his phone back.

"Why? So you can call her?! Fuck you!"

I took out his phone and threw it as far as I could. He then grabbed my phone from my hand and threw it. It was absolute insanity. We were both shaking and neither of us was in our right mind. We were radiating chaotic Whitney Houston/Bobby Brown energy and it was not cute. I kept asking THE question, the one I needed to know, the one I am sure you are dying to know too:

"DID YOU HAVE SEX WITH HER?!!"

"NO!" he exclaimed.

I didn't believe him. Not for a second. I thought maybe, if I asked him more slowly, he'd tell the truth.

"Did. You. Have. Sex. With. Her?!!!"

There was a pause. We stared at each other, still hyperventilating and on edge.

"We had oral. It was just a blow job."

JUST A BLOW JOB?! I went in for another swing and he ducked.

"It was nothing! It meant nothing!"

Our phones were lying shattered in the alleyway. He started telling me he wanted to kill himself. All the typical things a broken person says when they are caught. Anything to deflect from his part. He looked like he was losing his mind, and he was. Once I calmed down, I became the sane one in the relationship. Once again.

We drove to the Verizon store together to get our phones fixed. We were silent the entire way.

We didn't make up in the Verizon store and proceed to live happily ever after. We walked inside, both disheveled and Stephen sporting a massive slap print on his left cheek. We had "domestic dispute" written all over us. When the Verizon guy asked how both of our phones got cracked, I told him we were ambushed by ninjas. I don't think he bought it, but he did help fix our phones.

Later, with my good-as-new phone, I called Absolutely No Way, a.k.a. HEIDI, and confronted her. She broke down in tears, apologizing and saying she thought Stephen and I weren't in a good place. Apparently, that's what he'd told her. News to me! Although, looking back, we really weren't—he was high and I was deep in denial. Then I investigated/stalked her online and found that she was trying to move across town into our area??? That was it! I was done! I had to leave. Stephen broke down and admitted that he was not in his right mind, he was in his disease. It wasn't his true self; he was high and addicted . . .

Although that was all true, it does not make it right. I am not a doormat and you cannot walk all over me. He continued to say he didn't want to go on living if we weren't together, so I secretly planned my escape with my sponsor. I didn't want him to kill himself, and I knew he wasn't ready to hear that I was DONE. So I played it off like I forgave him and that we could work through it, when in reality I was looking for an apartment. Then a few weeks passed, and he came home crying. He grabbed my hands, looking like a sweet, terrified little boy who happened to be fucked up on Oxy . . . He said to me with more conviction than I had heard in months, "I'm done. I'm done. I'm done using. God spoke to me. I'm done!!!" Before I could respond, he RAN into his studio and grabbed the large box of pills that he kept in a metal lockbox, then proceeded to FLUSH them ALL down the toilet. Sorry, fish! (Or, you're welcome, fish?)

I talked more in depth about his detoxing in my first book, but a quick recap: Quitting cold turkey and detoxing from all of those heavy prescription drugs can kill you, and it nearly killed him. Thank God I took him to the hospital after he had flushed his pills, because he started seeing things that weren't there. Sweating and shaking, he turned to me, looking truly more terrified than I had ever seen him before, and said, "I see black clouds. They won't go away. They are looming over me. They are getting darker. So much black. Am I dying?" I immediately called someone in the program. I told them exactly what was happening and they said without hesitation, GET HIM TO THE HOSPITAL, NOW! So I did.

Within ten minutes of being there, he had a full-on seizure and his body went completely stiff. I screamed louder than I later would in childbirth and was taken away from the hospital room by several nurses. I was sure he had just died. They put me in a small room and attempted to comfort me while the doctors tried to resuscitate Stephen. Another nurse came back after the LONGEST ten minutes of my life and told me he was okay. If you're reading this and struggling with drug addiction or alcoholism, please detox medically when you're ready. Quitting cold turkey can kill you! I drove him straight from the hospital to a detox in Tarzana, deep in the San Fernando Valley.

From there, he went to a thirty-day all-male rehab. Meanwhile, I was still planning my escape. When he was in rehab and in a safe space, I told him I needed time and wanted to separate. He understood, though he was heartbroken. So was I. I never stopped loving him, but I never stopped loving myself either. I moved out for three months and he worked his steps as if his life depended on it. Over time, we healed. He showed me that he was sober and committed— to the point where he flew to Downers Grove, Illinois, to make amends to my parents. It was probably incredibly awkward, considering my father avoids any emotional talk like the plague. In fact, after Stephen was done reading them his heartfelt amends letter, apologizing for everything he had done to their daughter, my dad literally responded by saying, "You ever use earbuds at the gym? It's great to listen to some Led Zeppelin while you're lifting."

Want to know something else awkward? Of course you do! A couple of weeks after I screamed in a jealous rage, nearly smacking Stephen's deceitful head off, our neighbor knocked on the door. With an empathetic sigh, she handed me a well-worn book titled

Mating in Captivity. "I hope this isn't overstepping, but this book really helped us." It seems our arguments had not been subtle.

For many reasons, I was too scared to tell you about the affair in my first book. It's obviously hard to talk about. Even though I believe it's more common than we think, no one discusses it. I think there is a more severe stigma attached to addictions like sex and love than to alcohol or gambling. What makes it worse is that many people still do not believe that they are real. But the truth is, we can get addicted to anything. Sober alcoholics often develop cross-addictions to get that dopamine rush from new sources.

Obviously, I spoke to Stephen about putting this story in my book. He told me that it was okay because more people needed to talk about this, to remove the shame, embarrassment, and stigma around it. I thought it was incredibly brave of him to let me share it with you. I am still afraid of people judging him, or us . . . But hey, sober people (maybe all people) do best when we walk through fear and get rigorously, painstakingly honest with ourselves and others. My fear of judgment and shame around what happened just perpetuates the already harmful stigma.

AND ON THAT NOTE . . . the painstakingly honest one . . . I should probably confess that I haven't been a perfect angel either. Years ago, I had engaged in subtle flirtation with one or two guys online because the attention felt nice. They would DM me that they thought I was pretty and talented and I would say "thank you" rather than ignoring them. It opened up a line of communication that I eventually cut off. So, I understand the "high" one gets from feeling wanted and desired. It strokes the ego and gives you a rush of feel-good chemicals, which for sober people is like gold.

And one more thing . . . I may or may not have had an accidental "happy ending" at a Thai massage parlor years ago. LET ME EXPLAIN. It was during the time Stephen was on pills and our sex life was, well, nonexistent. I would get regular deep-tissue massages for forty dollars an hour at this little parlor down the road. One week, I met a new masseuse. She was beautiful and very strong. I told her she had magic hands and I started going to her regularly. One day during my deep-tissue rubdown, she got awfully close to my groin area. My breathing deepened and I couldn't help but become aroused. DID SHE KNOW WHAT SHE WAS DOING or was I just really horny? It was confusing! Then, she asked softly, "Does this feel good?" I paused for a minute and thought . . . *What does she mean by that? Is she flirting? Is this cheating? I'm so turned on right now . . . Should I tell her to stop? It feels so good, though . . . but it's just a massage, Laura,* I justified. And then I succumbed to the pleasure: "Yes. Yes, it feels good." She slowly moved closer to my sacred lady area . . . and continued rubbing faster (over the sheet, I should mention—or, does that even matter?). "Does *this* feel good?" she whispered again. I whispered-moaned back, "Yes. Yes." I was giving her the go-ahead to continue and continue she did. It was all-consuming and euphoric. Like, you know when you have to sneeze and you can sense it building up for a long time and then when you finally do and it is the most satisfying feeling in the world? It was like that. It was spellbinding the way she was able to make me peak over the sheet. I couldn't understand it. So I thought, *I should probably go back ONE more time and try to figure out what THAT was all about.* So I got one accidental happy ending and then another one on purpose. I haven't been perfectly faithful either. Progress, not perfection, right? I later admitted this to Stephen and instead of getting mad, he just got frisky.

And to back up my theory even further that there is no such thing as the perfect relationship, on my most recent accosting session with Anne, she was telling me about her partner of nearly fifty years. She admitted to me that he loved to gamble. When I asked how she dealt with that, to my surprise she responded, "I just kept giving him money." Then, she continued, "It wasn't all one-sided, though. I may have continued to give him money to support his habit, but he introduced me to the most fun people I have ever met. He believed that life was about pleasure and he gave me so much of it. I had the most fun times in my life because of that man." Anne chose to focus on what he did *right*.

Stephen and I have been together a decade now and I trust him. I trust *sober* Stephen. Though there is, on occasion, that little nagging fear in the back of my fidgety brain that thinks, *What if he slips? What if it happens again?* I've had to surrender this fear many times. Sometimes I ask him directly for reassurance that he will never hurt me like that again. But there are no guarantees in life other than death, so I try to stick to this mantra . . . which sounds kinda savage, but here it is:

> *It's him or something better. If we are meant to be, we will be. If not . . . something better. Always something better.*

I tell him from time to time, "I do not *need* you, Stephen. I want you and I love you with all of my heart. But if you deceive and betray me like this again, I'm on to something better."

Now more than ten years in, Stephen and I are both too exhausted from working and taking care of two small kids to even think about an affair. He's working his program, and I'm working mine. Not perfectly; it's progress. We argue, we cry, we laugh until we cry, we make love, we go on lots of walks, and we get better. We criticize each other and then motivate each other. We get annoyed with each other, then are in awe of each other. Most importantly, we giggle a lot. We still have so much fun together. Not every single day, but *a lot* of the time. We are supportive and creative together. And on the big stuff we mostly agree. There is truly not a dull moment in this relationship. Sometimes I wish there were! I truly believe that as long as we stay sober and our intentions are aligned, we will make it until the end. We'll be old and wrinkled, tits and balls down to our knees, making comedy sketches about our loss of elasticity—and still, hopefully, deeply devoted and in love.

I truly never stopped loving Stephen through all of this, but I also learned that I don't need him to be complete. Affairs are less forgivable for most people than a drug or alcohol relapse. IT JUST HURTS MORE! I get it. It's breaking a vow, whereas I don't think we vowed during our wedding ceremony never to snort a line . . . though we should have! "I ask you to take me as your devoted wife, for I will be loyal, a listening ear, and definitely not coked out of my brain, 'til death do us part."

I hope to help take the shame out of any sort of addiction or mental illness, which is why I'm telling these stories now. Anyone suffering from a physical illness would get treatment, and addiction is no different. It's a cunning, baffling, and powerful disease that affects the brain in profound ways. We fragile humans can get addicted to literally anything—drugs, alcohol, gambling, sugar, sex, food, shopping, work, or licking toads. (Seriously, google the last one. Or no, don't.) Work is a big one for me. I justify it because I feel my work is my calling and it's helping people, but I need to be consciously aware. I need to keep my sobriety and higher power first. Because if I'm addicted to work and then I get cancelled for accidentally using Demi Lovato's wrong pronouns, then I'm at risk for a relapse or mental breakdown . . . Right?

Instead of telling myself I *need* Stephen, I tell myself I *want* him. He is not my "other half." We are both two whole people who joined together to love, inspire, and bang each other. It feels FREEING to know that I am totally whole and I don't need ANY man or woman to complete me. This attitude actually makes Stephen more attracted to me. No one really wants to be *needed*, we want to be WANTED! It's good to know in my heart that I will always be okay. I've learned I cannot control him as much as I sometimes strive to. He is his own being with his own higher power and unique, beautiful path in this life. If we are meant to grow old together (which I REALLY hope we are), then we will. Now if I ask Stephen to go on a walk with me and he says no, I don't slip into a spiral of thinking it's over and he's a narcissist and I'll wind up living in a Motel 6 with my two kids. I just say "okay" and go on the walk by myself. I'll end up bumping into my ninety-eight-year-old guru, Anne, and she'll assure me that today is a gift and also to get the fuck out of her way, and it's absolutely beautiful. Just as it should be.

Now THAT is positive change.

CHAPTER 5

How Do I Fire Myself?

You probably already know that when an Indian jumping ant becomes a queen and reproduces, she loses up to 20 percent of her brain volume. This is common knowledge, right? You probably also know that they're the only species that can decrease *and then increase* their own brain size. They literally shed part of their brains to conserve energy, and then move that energy from their MINDS to their OVARIES. Well, that is nothing compared to the 98.8 percent of brain volume that I lose when I reproduce, and it definitely FELT like my ovaries ballooned to between five and fifteen times their normal size. Honestly, the ants have it easy. They can *regenerate* their lost brains once they have their babies. I have had two babies and I am running at 1.2 percent of my total brain capacity right now, and possibly forever. Maybe 1.3 percent right after I have caffeine, but that's it.

"But Laura, how do you do it all?" you might ask if you saw me breastfeeding while making a video while crying, while writing a book, falling apart, and forgetting to shower. And the answer is: I LITERALLY DON'T REMEMBER HOW I GOT INTO THIS ROOM!!!

When I found out I was pregnant with Alfie, I was of course thrilled about having my first baby. But I was equally terrified that pregnancy and motherhood would drain me not just of tit milk but of all my creativity. It would ruin me forever work-wise, socially, and emotionally. My front-butt was also a concern, but really, my creativity was what I most feared losing. Or maybe it was a tie. What if I never had an original or funny idea again, because half my brain was missing and the remaining half was figuring out how to keep a baby alive? I also had no idea what the future held for the characters I'd created, like Pamela Pupkin the Southern workout queen, or Ivy the vacant model (actually, with no brain cells I probably AM Ivy now). HOW was I going to make ALL of my characters pregnant? And what would become of square-faced mega-pervert Helen? Would she talk about eating Stephen's ass at the same time she was burping a baby? Or while she was at the pediatrician's, would she taunt Stephen about her pussy being like a juicy pork taco?

Becoming pregnant didn't kill my creativity, though. It made me tired and forgetful and slow to process complex philosophical questions like "How are you this morning?" But if anything, it changed my creativity for the better and helped me evolve. Getting pregnant was actually the best thing that's ever happened to my comedy. I went from doing absurd characters like Helen Horbath and Pamela Pupkin to writing sketches about my actual life, as a soon-to-be mother. My milk wagons weren't the only things swelling—so was my audience! As my body literally blew up in my pregnancy, so did my career.

Anyway, Helen was the character that put me on the map. She made millions of people laugh. They LOVED her inappropriate, lewd, totally ridiculous seduction techniques. What I love most about Helen is her totally uncalled-for confidence. In my mind, she's from a dysfunctional family of barely working-class stoners in the suburbs of Chicago, but in *her* mind she's Beyoncé. I knew Helen was something special when a fan got a tattoo of her permanently inked into his arm (I wonder if sometimes, late at night, he regrets it?). Eventually, I admit even I became tired of perverted puns, cheesy one-liners, and using a Snapchat filter that I didn't even own. Helen was completely dependent on this filter that could be taken away from me at any minute. That's really what prompted me to animate her. But before the animation idea, I thought that maybe *I* could become the animated Helen.

To make that (horrifying) transformation happen, I met with some big-time prosthetic artist guy. He tried to create Helen's square face for me so I wouldn't have to depend on the Snapchat filter to become that character. I went to his creepy/incredible house in Simi Valley, which was full of foam masks and scary *Nutty Professor*–type appendages. He covered my face in strange, suffocating materials until I could barely breathe—but I will do anything for my art. I will bleed, sweat, cry tears, and—apparently—willingly suffocate to death.

Being covered up like that was scary, but not as petrifying as the moment I looked in the mirror and saw Helen staring back at me. Actually, it was more like a horror movie version of Helen where she ate people's faces off and *then* talked about rim jobs. In other words, it was not quite right . . . at all. To this day, I still occasionally find pieces of Helen's foam cheeks or spongy chin in my bathroom drawers. I guess I should clean, but who has time for that? I have a life to live, in bed, with the blankets pulled over my head.

So when I saw how horrifying I looked, the prosthetic idea died of fright. That's when *actual* animation became the next step.

I got some meetings and pitched my animated Helen idea to some network executives as the female *Family Guy*. Seriously, there hasn't been a successful female-driven animation since . . . *DARIA?* COME ON! I explained that it would be irreverent and hilarious and would follow Helen and her barely working-class family of women. Her square face was perfect for TV screens. Well, that pitch was about three years ago! Now Alfie is over two years old and I had a whole second kid, and the show is *just* starting to get made with CBS Studios. Maybe if I have another kid and that kid graduates from high school, they'll start animating the first episode. That's how long it takes for anything to get made in Hollywood. Two full pregnancies plus a lifetime.

Anyway, I had built my career on playing absurd characters, but when I became pregnant, I decided to make a massive pivot. I would write about what was right in front of me instead: my big fat fucking belly. Getting knocked up opened up a whole new world of content, and even though I said goodbye to all those characters for the time being, I know Helen is out there masturbating in a dingy basement somewhere. And Pamela is doing some unintentionally sexual infomercial for a two-fisted Shake Weight. I'm forever grateful to Helen, since she opened up so many doors and legs for me and basically put her name (and my name) on the viral video map. Those doors swing both ways, and she is still out there, horny and waiting for her big comeback. So stay tuned . . .

For a long time, I assumed that what people loved about *me* was

Helen (or Pamela or Ivy), and I guess I was afraid that without those characters, no one would watch my videos. But the joke was on me! I have made my biggest viral videos yet writing about my real-life experiences. Bigger than Helen, bigger than Pamela, bigger than Ivy—writing about my actual life has resonated with so many more people. It makes sense, really—I'm writing about an experience universal to millions of women.

I'm not gonna lie—the idea of "mom comedy" made me cringe initially. I thought I was *for sure* going to lose my "cool factor." I'M NOT A REGULAR MOM, I'M A COOL MOM, OKAY?!

Before I was really "showing," when I was three or four months pregnant with Alfie, Facebook gave me a ONE-MILLION-DOLLAR budget to shoot a Pamela Pupkin pilot (no, they did not pay *me* a million dollars, but the total budget for the pilot was about a million). I was used to making Pamela workout videos for about five hundred dollars total. A chunk of that was spent on Pamela's aerobics tights, leotards, and on hiring Alan, the eighty-four-year-old actor I found on an L.A. casting website who became like the grandfather I never had. In the '70s, Alan was a second assistant director on movies like *Rosemary's Baby*, and he decided in *his* seventies to become an actor. Now he is the star of all the Pamela Pupkin workout videos! He is the perfect example of the fact that it is never too late to do what you love. He is an inspiration, and maybe I should set him up with Anne before it's too late? Yes, I will definitely be doing that.

Here I was, making my very own mega-budget Facebook pilot! It was supposed to be a fake talk show but with real guests, like Larry Sanders meets Borat. Pamela was the host and she interviewed actual people in the "healthy living space" (because that's a thing), but they wouldn't know she was a character. So I hid my four-month-pregnant belly with a 1980s pink and white windbreaker customized with "PAMELA" written on the back in rhinestones, and we shot the pilot, which I thought was going to be my *Star Wars*. It was going to be my million-dollar MOMENT. Turns out, I was right—it was my moment, because that's exactly how long the show lasted.

The Facebook executives decided to stop by the set one day to see how their million-dollar budget was being spent. One of the people I cast in the Pamela pilot (besides eighty-four-year-old Alan, who played the security guard who was always either sleeping or accidentally discharging his gun) was a Vietnamese woman named Eve. I'd met her at a coffee shop on Hollywood Boulevard one day. She was tiny (three foot seven) and adorable, and she had kyphosis, which means a curved spine. I loved everything about her. Because I have zero impulse control, I approached her and told her I thought she looked amazing. She looked up at me in shock and then said in the sweetest voice with a very thick accent, "Nobody ever says I'm amazing!" I was instantly in love. I asked her to be in my workout video, which I was filming the next day. It was going to star interesting people of all ages, shapes, and sizes. She said yes! In true Hollywood fashion, though, she became a diva faster than you can say *Cher*.

She started demanding I pay her more money for each video she was in and that I only pay her in cash. What a fucking legend! Anyway, I convinced Facebook executives to let me cast her in the role of Pamela's assistant in the million-dollar pilot. I should also mention that she barely speaks any English, which didn't matter to me. The director struggled because of it, but I didn't care. So the day that the executives came to watch, we were filming a scene where Pamela gets pissed because Eve tried to murder her. Eve did this by running Pamela over with her motorized cubicle (stay with me here). So Pamela, in self-defense, kicks Eve's motorized cubicle. And, well . . . this sounds really bad as I'm writing it . . . she knocks down a disabled woman. Eve was fine! She thought it was hilarious! AND SHE WAS TRYING TO MURDER PAMELA—IT WAS SELF-DEFENSE! It was also probably the most offensive scene in the whole million-dollar pilot, and of course that's what the frowning suits saw.

They also got to see a scene where Stephen, who played Roger, Pamela's painfully submissive husband, was facing toward a wall, frantically cleaning mustard off the crotch area of his khakis. It looked as though he were aggressively masturbating. Pamela walked in: "WHAT THE FUCK, ROGER!? STOP WIGGLING YOUR YOGURT HOSE IN MY FUCKIN' OFFICE!" My comedy is very highbrow, ambitious, cutting-edge—avant-garde, really! But the executives couldn't see that. They just saw advertisers running away clutching *their* millions of dollars. No sane brand would go near this show. I probably should have thought about that before writing the most offensive comedy of all time.

The pilot didn't get picked up. Are you surprised? I actually kinda was. Okay, I was fucking devastated. I put so much work and energy into that project, and it went down faster than a disabled woman in a motorized cubicle. Looking back, though, it was actually the best thing that could have happened to me. If the Pamela pilot had gone to series and turned into a show, I would have been driving an hour every morning to Hollywood to write and film and edit a show for fourteen hours a day, while very pregnant. And then I would get to continue to do it all with a NEWBORN. I would have missed the most incredible moments with my new, beautiful baby, Alfie. I would have had to stress about childcare and pumping rooms and boobs leaking on set.

As soon as I was finished being devastated, that's when I started filming sketches about my *real* life, and what I was really going through. And then everything changed! After the studio executives told me to fuck off (but also please keep posting to our platform!), I once again had total creative freedom. I was able to work from home and make my own hours (my shoots while pregnant would never exceed four hours, because my feet and back hurt and I kept pissing myself). And when I had my son, I got to continue to film at home, with total creative freedom, filming around his nap and feeding schedules. I could take breastfeeding and play breaks whenever I wanted. I didn't miss a moment with him. IT WAS FUCKING AMAZING and I am incredibly grateful.

I've always made these grand plans for myself. In this case, those plans involved thinking a fancy million-dollar pilot was my destiny. But then God or the universe had another plan. And it was so much better. Oftentimes, or dare I say *every* time, it's better than anything I could have imagined. This perceived "failure" was one of the best things to ever happen to me. It helped me develop my voice as an artist and even to write beyond comedy. Because I wasn't in the studio all day filming for a show I didn't even own, I got to write and film things that really meant something to me, without any gatekeepers in my way. I even started making (intentionally) unfunny content about worthy causes that mean something to me, like normalizing breastfeeding. Once again, I took control of my career. The executives said "no," so I made my own show from my living room. It was MY authentic voice, without a bunch of executives watering it down. And—get this—I made more money filming my own ideas from my iPhone than I would have if the show had been picked up!

This is one of the reasons I LOVE social media. Now is the BEST time to be an artist or business owner or creator of any kind! We have global distribution at our FINGERTIPS. Just you and a phone and a dream. For years, starting when I was eighteen years old and going out on auditions for projects I had no say in or control over, I had gatekeepers telling me, "NO, you're too tall/short/young/ old/loud/quiet/intense/bland/bug-eyed/sexy/drunk/sober . . . NEXT!!!" Usually I booked just enough work to keep a roof over my head, crackers in my pantry, and drugs in my system. It wasn't THE life, but it was *a* life. Anyway, about ten years in, I had an audition for a show that I actually loved. The part was well-written and I finally had a chance to do something that I believed in. I felt like it was the next *Friends* and I would be the next Phoebe. I am telling you, it was incredible. A once-in-a-career-type role. I do not remember what it was called or what it was about, but I remember it being *amazing*.

I went on my third callback, which means the producers like you and keep asking you to drive out to audition AGAIN. It's amazing but also completely anxiety-provoking. I figured this was my big moment, because THREE callbacks! I memorized twelve pages of script, and I made Stephen rehearse with me until both of our brains exploded.

On the third audition, I had several scenes to read. I nailed the first scene and paused, ready for the casting director to either say, "That was incredible, you're hired!" or at a minimum, "Wonderful, Laura, let's move on to the next scene now." Instead, very dryly, with a noticeably insincere smile on her face, she said, "Thank you for coming in." Her smile faded and the silence was loud.

In audition speak, "thank you for coming in" translates to: "You did not get the job. We have no use for you anymore, you desperate little attention whore. You may as well go back to the tiny midwestern suburb whence you came. NEXT!" That's the literal translation.

Normally I would have chirped, "Okay, thank you SO much for taking the time to see me. Oh, and I love your tweed blazer! Bye-bye!" Then I would have left the audition room reeking of desperation, only to go home and berate myself for being too tall/short/young/old/loud/quiet/intense/bland/bug-eyed/sexy/drunk/sober. But I had been auditioning for SO many years and I finally hit my breaking point. I looked her dead in the eyes and instead of kissing her ass like most actors do because we have no other option—since the casting directors have all the power in the relationship—I said nicely . . .

"Can you tell me what I did wrong?"

She paused and then looked up from her phone, SHOCKED. How DARE I ask her for feedback and not just exit her office with my obsessively highlighted and notated script tucked between my legs? Her tight smile grew angrier and she repeated in a slow, condescending tone, "Thank you . . . for coming in."

But her eyes? They screamed *GET THE FUCK OUT, you Dollar Tree Kristen Wiig!*

But I didn't budge.

"I just want to know what I did wrong," I said. "It would be really helpful to me to know what I could have done better. Or if I just wasn't right for the role?"

She stared at me like she was *so* offended that I was ACTUALLY SPEAKING WORDS AT HER that weren't in the script. I continued anyway, knowing she'd probably never invite me back for another audition.

"Was I too intense? Not intense enough? Too tall? I am a giant, but a friendly one! Is it my overbite? Because I think it gives me character—also my parents couldn't afford to get me braces. Is that why I didn't get the part, because my parents couldn't afford braces? Or maybe you've offered the role to Mandy Moore? Just tell me. I just want to know. Did you offer the role to Mandy Moore? I won't be mad. I loved her 1999 hit song 'Candy'! I mean, looking back, I'd say the lyrics are a little too sexual for a teen, but still undeniably catchy!"

Then I started reciting the lyrics to "Candy," which didn't help the situation.

"I'm missing you like candaaay, yeah yeahhhh—I JUST WANT TO KNOW WHAT I DID WRONG!"

I was so angry that this amazing pilot, which I was SO confident I was going to book, was passing me by. My dreams were being put on hold once again. My life was 99 percent rejection and I just couldn't understand it. I knew I was funny; I knew I was meant to do this. WHY DIDN'T SHE KNOW THIS? I needed answers and I deserved answers. Anything would have been fine: constructive criticism, acknowledgment, respect, anything. Her irritation increased and she repeated in a truly menacing tone, "*Thank you . . . for coming in.*"

"You're a fucking cunt!" I screamed back, and then I punched her in her titties! I wish that were true. Instead I walked out silently, embarrassed, defeated, with my crinkled script tucked between my chicken legs.

But seriously, what a fucking cunt! All I wanted to do was make the world laugh the way I made my friends laugh growing up. It's one of the things I believe I was created to do and they weren't letting me do it! To feel like I couldn't fulfill my life's purpose . . .

well, it was the most frustrating thing in the world for me. I was depressed. I even thought about killing myself. Looking back, I just didn't understand my power yet.

After that, the last audition I EVER went out for was a comedy pilot and the role went to Brooklyn Decker. Yet again I was beside myself! It was another one I was SURE I was going to get. Brooklyn is way more gorgeous than I am, but I am funnier than she is! I think even *she'd* agree on that—she's hotter, I'm funnier! Still, she got the role.

I am one of those weirdos who believes that my higher power has a plan (maybe because surrender helps me sleep better) and that all of those perceived failures were not really failures at all. They were perfectly preparing me for where I am today. Because I read literally thousands of scripts day and night for YEARS, I learned how to write and perform comedy in the process. Those ten years prepared me to make the content I make today. I put in my 10,000 hours. I always imagined I'd be on *SNL* or on the next *Friends,* but what I have is SO MUCH BETTER. Total creative freedom— I don't have to get my script approved by anyone. I can just make a fucking song about fucking potatoes. I don't mean a song about literally having intercourse with potatoes, although I COULD DO THAT IF I WANTED TO. Maybe someone *should* stop me once in a while, but too bad, because I have no boss! I am the boss. I have tried to fire myself many, many times, but it never takes.

LAURA: "Laura, come into my office, please."

LAURA: "You mean your bed, because that's where we do most of our work, you depressed, procrastinating whore."

LAURA: "Don't talk to me like that . . . I'm your boss!"

LAURA: "Wow, in that case we're really fucked, aren't we?"

LAURA: "HAHAHA, yeah, what were we thinking?"

LAURA: "No one else would hire us?"

LAURA: "That's true. Hey, we should probably masturbate for a quick minute. Get our creative juices flowing, if you know what I mean?"

LAURA: "You're funny, but it's 2021 and you can't suggest that to your employees anymore."

For too many years I had a limiting belief that I was just this funny puppet who could say other people's words and make them hilarious, but I didn't trust my own voice or my own writing. I talked about this in my first book, and about walking through that fear to create something greater and more fulfilling than I could have imagined. Before, if a sitcom I was on sucked, it wasn't my fault. I didn't write it! Now, if something is bad there is no one to blame but myself, which is freeing and also terrifying. Making comedy about my own life was a risk, because if people "hate it" they essentially "hate me." Even hiding behind characters was easier, because it wasn't really me. But I swear, the bigger the risk, the greater the payoff.

One smoggy morning during my serenity stroll, I bumped into Saint Anne and casually asked her what her most important piece of life advice was. Without hesitation, she said, "Individual responsibility. Never run away from working on yourself. Your life is in *your* hands." My life was in MY hands, not the cunty casting director's.

The more vulnerable I became with my content, the more my career blossomed and the more positive effects I had on my audience. I was not just able to make millions of people around the world laugh, which was always my goal, but also to talk about real issues—like mental health, addiction, social injustice, and postpartum depression. By doing that, I let women know they're not alone. I also learned that "mom comedy" is not the niche I assumed it was. *Most* women become mothers, 43.5 million to be exact-ish. If that's a niche, then my name is Brooklyn Decker, and my name is NOT Brooklyn Decker because I did NOT book that pilot.

One day when I was stressing about losing my creativity and having my career tank because I was bringing a life into this world, I pissed all over myself. That one pregnancy "trickle" changed the course of my life forever. As the pee was coursing down my swollen legs I realized, hey, unintentionally pissing myself because I sneezed is funny. And I make funny videos for a living. So why not make a funny video about pregnancy in all its disgusting glory *right now?* And so I did, and here we are.

As amazing as it has been making that transition to creating comedy about my actual life, there are days when I feel immense guilt for sometimes prioritizing my work over my kids. I know so many parents experience this guilt, and if you guys have advice about how to make it go away, please tell me! I sometimes feel like a sociopathic demon (a minor one, not on the level of a casting director) when Alfie is knocking on my office door and I'm on a conference call and I can't immediately open it and comfort him. Stephen and I are both extremely passionate about creating art, and it can at times be all-consuming. We are also extremely passionate about our children, and the balancing act can feel as challenging as walking a tightrope over the Grand Canyon. IT'S JUST AS CHALLENGING AS THAT, you guys.

I often yearn to be in two places at once. Working from home while having two small children who *also* need my time, tits, and attention is still a challenge I haven't yet mastered. If you came to this book looking for the answer to that question, sorry! I have other wonderful qualities like my double-jointed thumb, but juggling work and motherhood is something I am still figuring the fuck out.

My mom was always home with us 24/7 and I loved it. She tutored kids with learning disabilities in our living room, so I never had to wonder where she was or when she'd be back—she was always RIGHT THERE. I want my kids to have that same sense of safety and security, but I ALSO want to work. I LOVE my work. And I LOVE being a mom. I'm still navigating the balance. Hopefully, watching Stephen and me living our dreams will encourage our kids to discover what it is that makes their hearts sing, whether it's painting or accounting. All I wish for is that my kids are able to identify and nurture their own unique gifts, know that it's possible to do what they love, and also not be giant dickheads.

I do love that when I post videos now about being a mom, millions of women are like, "ME FUCKIN' TOO!" It's so wonderful to connect on this wild experience with all of you, and the more content I create around it, the more convinced I am that we are all more or less living the same lives. I don't think I've ever had a unique thought. Like when I posted that being with my children is incredible but when they both are asleep it's even more incredible. You don't judge me, but repeatedly let me know, "Me fuckin' too!" That connection helps me feel less guilty about stepping away from my kids to make videos about engorged milk wagons. I know there are some people who really miss my old content, the pickup lines and Helen's horniness. People don't like change, but I have changed—eight thousand diapers and counting! And I have changed as a human being, too, thank God. (But also—Helen is NOT DEAD, she's just evolving . . .)

I could not have done any of this without the help of Carla, our incredible, loving, kind, alarmingly patient nanny. I met Carla because her mom, Elousia, has been our housekeeper for over a decade. Elousia left a challenging household in Guatemala for a better life, and she's been in *our* life since Stephen and I were in our first one-bedroom apartment. She had Carla when she was twenty-two years old and was living in Koreatown in L.A. Carla started off as my part-time assistant, and one day I asked if she'd be willing to help out with Alfie. Carla started telling me how passionate she is about children, and how it's her dream to open her own day care one day (something I intend to assist her with in any way I can). She has been the most incredible nanny and loves our kids, more than I do sometimes. They absolutely adore her. She's Alfie's best friend and we don't know what we'd do without her. When she is not here, I'm in the kitchen with a baby on my tit, trying to do a one-handed edit of my comedy sketch while being accosted for snacks by my willful toddler. I am thankful for Carla every damn day she comes.

One day when I was overwhelmed with work and kids and just feeling like I needed to get the fuck out, I went on one of my "five minutes to fulfillment" walks. (I fully realize how cheesy I've become and I do not care.) Because Anne and I were destined to be in each other's lives (according to me), there she appeared. She was marching with her gleaming silver cane in hand as if she were a magical sorceress, which she is. I power-walked up to her and said hello. Because I can tell her anything (whether she asks or not), I told her about how stressful, exasperating, even maddening it felt at times having a two-month-old *and* a two-year-old. She just looked at me with empathy and compassion and nodded.

I asked Anne if she had any kids of her own. Since she was so nurturing by nature, I assumed the answer would be: yes, twelve of them. Well, I was wrong. Anne suddenly looked wistful.

"No," she said quietly. "I don't have any kids. It's the biggest regret of my life, not having children. As a little girl I couldn't wait to be a mom, and I would tell my own mother all the time that I wanted to one day have two boys and two girls, but that didn't happen." Anne said she never married, was always working, and was well into her forties by the time she met the man she wanted to settle down with.

Tears filled her eyes. There was a long pause and I was unsure of what exactly to say. Then Anne filled the silence. "I have no idea where I'd be or how my life would have turned out if I'd had children," she said. "I certainly would not be who I am today." We looked into each other's eyes, each with slight envy for the other. I envied her ninety-eight years of total freedom and uninterrupted sleep, and she craved having children to love. Then it felt as though in that moment, we both made peace with our decisions.

"And that's enough complaining from me," she said matter-of-factly. "It was nice to see you, Laura." Then Anne the suburban sorceress continued her trudge down the steep hill as I trudged up. Anne graciously sharing her biggest regret inspired me once again to get back into a state of gratitude for all that I have. Especially my children, no matter how annoying they can be.

Surprisingly, becoming a mom actually made me more productive for the most part. Before kids, waking up at ten in the morning was EARLY for me, and also, what is structure? I was once so undisciplined and chaotic that actually sticking to a routine . . . well, it never happened (I do blame my ADHD for this). But now I'm up at the ass-crack of dawn and routine is *everything*. With kids, I have no choice but to stick to a schedule, AND IT'S AMAZING. My kids have made me realize that I am capable of more than I ever thought. Lucille Ball once said, "The more you do, the more you can do." I love this. I love Lucy!

I know not every parent can work from home or have a nanny. I also know not every parent *wants* these things. There's always been an unrealistic expectation that women should just "handle it," and by "it" I mean ALL OF IT. When I first left Alfie with Carla, as much as I loved and trusted her, I was terrified and guilt-ridden. It's scary just handing your child to someone and walking out the door. That first time, Alfie was four or five months old. I was flying on a private jet to Sweden for a movie. Wait—no, that's not accurate. I was going on a walk around the block. But it FELT like I was flying on a private jet to Sweden for a movie. As I handed over my firstborn, I was like, "Okay, great. I'm going out. On a walk. Here's my child . . ."

"Okay, have fun," Carla said.

"Call or text me!" I said.

"I will. Have fun!"

"Just . . . call or text me if anything happens while I'm walking around this block."

"Okay."

"Call or text me!"

"Yeah . . . you said that!"

Then I left, and immediately texted Carla to make sure she knew to call or text me if I needed to come back. I was so nervous during that whole walk. I was worrying about things like what if Alfie misses me, or what if he's hungry, or what if he resents me forever and has to go through years of intense therapy because I went on that walk around the block?! I obsessed about this for the entire endless five minutes. Then I walked back into the house and saw Carla bottle-feeding a perfectly content Alfie. With Penelope, my second baby, it's easier. Getting through those first few times leaving your child is tough, but now I lateral Penelope over to Carla like a football: "Catch!"

I still add "call me or text me," but during my walks I can talk to Anne or just enjoy the walk and feel relaxed(ish). I don't know if she's an easier baby or I'm just a less anxious mom now. But my point is, I am thankful every day that I can trust Carla with my babies and get work done and go on a much-needed stroll. The only issues are when Carla says things like, "She almost crawled today!" That's when I'm like, "WOW, this one walk RUINED my life!" Missing a milestone is devastating! But then I take a breath and remind my psycho brain that it is okay and life will go on even if I miss her first, adorably slithery "*almost crawl.*"

CHAPTER 6

Me Too, Though
(a.k.a. Stories I Was Too Scared
to Tell in My First Book)

I wrote an entire book called *Idiot* in which I shared my most mortifying experiences. I opened up about my coke addiction and my relationship with a psychotic, abusive drug dealer. I told you about the time I went to work while tripping balls on magic mushrooms. In my social media I've posted intimate, graphic videos showing the births of BOTH of my kids, which have been viewed by 80 million people and counting. I filmed my postpartum depression, and I make sure to fill you in on all the gruesome details of motherhood. By now, you probably know more about my psychological profile and my lady-taco than you ever wanted to. But there are still some personal stories I have not told before because I was too scared.

But not anymore.

Think of this chapter as an intermission, and a chance to sit back, relax, and cringe as you wonder out loud what the fuck was wrong with me. Hopefully these stories will make you feel better about your life decisions.

Let's just get right into it . . .

I drugged my own sister, Colleen. And I don't mean with a pot brownie. It's one of the MOST shameful, horrific things I have ever done, if not *the* most shameful, horrific thing, so you can probably see why I left it out of my first book. Why am I telling you now? Because one day, I was going on and on to my sister about how nerve-racking it was to release a book with such intimate personal stories. She looked at me, squinted a bit, and said, "Hmm . . . right."

"Excuse me?" I said, taken aback. "'Hmm . . . right'? Do you know how hard it is to share my life with the world? All of my failures?"

She looked unimpressed. "I mean, I did notice you left out the story of when you drugged me."

I paused. Fuck, she was right. "Yeah, . . . I did. I guess I'm scared. I'm scared they'll hate me if I tell them."

"I don't hate you, Laura, and I'm the one you drugged."

That was all I needed to hear. So, here it goes:

When I was eighteen years old and living in Los Angeles, my mom called and told me that my grandma was dying and I needed to get home to Downers Grove immediately. That might sound perfectly normal, except that it was a total lie. To her credit, she told me this massive and potentially traumatizing lie to get me away from an abusive relationship with a guy named Damon, so she was actually being kind—and it worked. I had an excuse to escape Damon's demonic clutches. A few years later, my mom called to tell me that my grandma had died. I was like, "Ha ha ha . . . Mom, I'm not even *with* Damon anymore."

"No, seriously, Laura, Grandma's gone."

There was silence and then a sniffle. This time I knew she was telling the truth.

Colleen, who was by this point living in L.A. with me, loved our grandma Alice as much as I did. Alice was easy to love. Just imagine for a minute the kindly appearance of Mrs. Claus and the demeanor of Mother Teresa . . . THAT was my lovable grandma Alice. Her only flaw was that she didn't think homosexuality was a real thing. No one's perfect, right? So to honor her memory and ease our pain, we decided to go out that very night and get completely fucked up off our tits at the Mondrian Hotel on Sunset Boulevard. We didn't have any money, but the Mondrian was always crawling with sleazy rich assholes dying to buy drinks for young, broke, beautiful women. We knew we could get as drunk as we wanted for free, and we needed to get numb. Grandma Alice would have approved.

Just like we'd predicted, we met two creepy old guys (in their thirties!) who seemed cool enough, so we let them buy us drinks. One of them was an actor whom I'll call Jared. If I showed you his photo you'd go, "Oh, I know that face . . . He's in that one cop show, right? Or was it the thriller where the landlord hides under Jessica Biel's bed? Was that it?" Eh, doesn't matter, I'll take a vodka soda with four limes, please. We told Jared and his friend that we were mourning our sweet grandmother and they convincingly seemed to care (acting, my dear!). They invited us to dinner at Dan Tana's, which is an old-school West Hollywood Italian restaurant with red-and-white-checkered tablecloths and photos of Frank Sinatra on the walls. This was in my pre-vegan years, so I probably ordered a steak medium rare. Back then if I was getting a free dinner, I was not fucking around with a wedge salad.

As we continued to get sloppy drunk, Jared slurred, "Hey, we have this drug that makes you feel amazing if you want to try it." I immediately said yes—to any drug offer, ever. Because I'm a sucker for treasuring romantic details, I asked what it was.

"GHB," Jared said.

"Sounds amazing!" I slurred back. I had no idea what it was.

I asked what it stood for and Jared's friend said, "Gamma-hydroxybutyrate."

"OMG . . . the *G* stands for GAMMA! We have to take this, Colleen. This is a sign. In honor of Gamma Alice!" Colleen looked at me like I was batshit crazy . . . because I was.

What I didn't know then was that GHB was also known as the "date rape" drug.

"I'll take some!" I said naively. "Gamma for Gramma!"

Colleen said she didn't want any. I took some and waited for it to kick in, and we continued eating medium-rare cow. Later, when Colleen went to the bathroom and I was starting to feel pretty fucking amazing, Jared and his friend were like, "We should slip some in her drink."

Being the loving, thoughtful younger sister that I am, I enthusiastically responded, "That's a fantastic idea! She'll love this! She'll *totally* thank me later . . ."

And just like that, I poured a little splash into her champagne. I date-rape-drugged my own sister.

In my defense, I had no clue it was a date-rape drug! In my addict mind I thought, "Colleen just doesn't understand how great she's going to feel and so I'm going to help her out." I know now it's twisted and SO fucked up, but at the time I felt like I was doing her a favor. Like I was introducing her to hot yoga or dill pickle almonds (they're delicious, I swear). Colleen came back to the table and I kept drinking and pretending everything was normal while she finished her spiked champagne. Yes to sisterhood!

After dinner, Colleen said she was feeling tired (oops!), and she asked us to drop her off at home since we were going out to some club where Leonardo DiCaprio *definitely* was. When she was getting out of the car she heard Jared say, "Oh man, it didn't work." She turned back toward us and asked, "What didn't work?" I quickly came clean about putting GHB in her drink. Or maybe Jared told her. She almost *too* casually shook her head and then walked inside. It's almost like she wasn't that shocked that I would do something like this—which tells you a lot about what a shitty (but also sick) individual I was at the time. Hey, she must not have been THAT mad, because she ended up going out to see a band with a friend of hers and, *in her words*, she had a "fucking great night." So she actually did thank me in the end! I mean, not out loud, BUT SHE HAD A GREAT NIGHT, with zero rape involved.

While Colleen was out dancing with her girlfriend, I had an insane night with Jared the character actor and his friend whose name I can't remember. I also don't remember much of the night, but I do remember that we went to Jared's place and continued drinking, and he pulled out a ginormous box of about a thousand pills of molly. I didn't take all one thousand pills, but I took at least one.

Anyway, I woke up the next morning to see Jared's friend standing over me with a tray of pancakes and fresh orange juice he'd squeezed himself. Just kidding. I woke up to see him masturbating right over my face with a demonic look in his eyes.

I immediately went into survival mode. My mind quickly started racing to stay alive. If this man whose name I could not remember was capable of sexual assault, would he rape and murder me? If I screamed, would he knock me unconscious and sell me into sexual slavery? Neither of those seemed like a good option, so I did what any street-smart nineteen-year-old coming off a bender would do: I froze and let him finish. And then I casually pretended I had to go home and I bolted out the front door.

This was in the pre-#MeToo era—the first six thousand years of human civilization when, sadly, women were way too used to these things happening. We were usually quiet about it because we were ashamed or we thought we'd get blamed or we actually believed it was our fault. So I went home and didn't even tell Colleen about it. I was completely disgusted and sad and humiliated. When I walked into our apartment, Colleen, who I thought was going to hate me, said, "Girl, I had the best night ever!" So at least one of us didn't wake up with a strange dick in her face! Karma? What's that and how does it work?

Whatever it was, off to Gamma's funeral we went.

I wish I could say that was the first time something like that happened to me, but I can't. When I was fifteen years old, I went with some older friends to a house party in Downers Grove. We had some beer and weed, and since my tolerance was so low, I got completely fucked up and could barely walk. There was a basement in the house that had a bed in it, so one of them took me down there and told me to take a nap, while a bunch of other teenagers got wasted upstairs. What could go wrong?

I woke up to see a massive nineteen-year-old unzipping my pants and attempting to pull them down. I knew he was about to rape me. I could tell this by instinct, but also by the look in his eyes: desperate and vacant and savage all at once. I'll never forget the sound of his breath, aggressively panting through his mouth like an attack dog, right above me. He hadn't yet noticed my eyes were open. And just like I would years later at Jared's house, I went into survival mode and froze. I scanned the room. It was dark and cold, with only one way out. I could hear the distant muffled chatter of drunk teens upstairs, music playing, drinks clinking on tables. How was I going to escape? No one could hear me, and this guy was double my size.

As I was scanning the basement for a weapon or an escape route, he looked right into my eyes. He saw that I was no longer passed out. I was awake and looking right at him. My jeans were halfway down my legs at this point. I was so terrified I was almost numb. He looked so angry that I had woken up, truly sick in the head—deranged—like a wild animal in a trap. Before he could act, I decided to play it off like I was into this. It was the only thing I could think of. It's amazing how the brain comes up with solutions so quickly when we're in fight-or-flight mode. Hiding my absolute terror, I said in a flirty yet shaken voice, "Oh, hey. . ." He was still breathing heavily, and my pants were now at my ankles.

I scanned the room again, but the only escape was out that one door and up the dirty carpeted stairs. I could see a glimpse of light through the bottom of the door, and I knew I had to get to the other side. He didn't have to say anything because his eyes told me very clearly that if I tried to get up, there would be trouble. I barely knew him (to be clear, I knew his name, but I am giving him the undeserved courtesy of leaving it out). He was five years older than me and grew up in our neighborhood. The heavy breathing continued, and I could feel it on my neck, hot and revolting. His face was so close to mine. I continued acting like I was unfazed by what was about to happen, when really I was screaming inside.

Then I managed to say, in a soft whisper, "I just have to pee—I'll be *right* back."

He pivoted his giant sweaty body off me, just enough so I could move. He bought it. I couldn't believe it! I quickly pulled my pants back up as I ran faster than I ever had in my entire life. I flew up the dark basement stairs toward the light, praying that the door wouldn't somehow be locked, and it wasn't. I opened the door, hysterically shaking and crying.

I found my (sort of) friends and told them, through my tears, what happened. My heart raced and my stomach was in knots. They comforted me, but we were so young and none of us had a clue what to do. We were too scared, afraid WE would be the ones to get in trouble. I never reported what happened. Staying quiet seemed like a better option than reporting an assault, at the time. I'm telling you, the pre-#MeToo years were *fucked up*.

Okay, that's enough sexual assault stories. Oh . . . you disagree and want more? WELL, YOU'RE IN LUCK THEN!!!

Take the time I was assaulted *again*, this time by the brother of a very famous actor. Let's just call him Lance (the brother, not the actor). I was living in an apartment in a white Craftsman house on Holloway Drive that Marilyn Monroe used to live in when she was still Norma Jean. This fact made me the talk of my hometown, Downers Grove, Illinois, for *at least* a full week. The most glamorous part of this shared address, for me, was the fact that I peed in the same toilet as Marilyn Monroe. Every time I peed, I felt like Hollywood royalty. I couldn't get over it. Some people might feel special because they slept in the same bedroom as Marilyn or had the same garden, but not me. My ass and Marilyn's ass were one.

One day when I was out doing my usual—that is, getting

fucked up—I met Lance, who immediately started name-dropping and talking about his ultra-famous brother. Lance was a cool guy (or so I thought), a total bad boy, and we became friends. Until the morning I woke up to find Lance raping me. Again, I froze. I knew that if I resisted, he might kill me. My logic again was simply that if you're capable of rape, you're capable of murder. I was scared for my life. I lay there frozen in terror as he continued to abuse me; I pretended that I was still asleep. To make matters worse, I never confronted him. I never told anyone. I JUST PRETENDED IT NEVER HAPPENED. I was too ashamed and scared. I felt like it was somehow my fault. I shouldn't have been sleeping on the couch that night. I should have never flirted with him. I shouldn't have been drinking. The shame was too great for me to tell anyone. I didn't even tell my sister, let alone report him to the police. I knew it would be his word—and maybe his famous brother's word—against mine. So I never reported him. I never told anyone until now.

In case you've detected a pattern and you're wondering—yes, all of the stories I was too scared to tell involve unwelcome penises. All except one story, which we'll get to in a little bit. For now, let's continue with the unwanted dicks . . .

There was also the time I was lured to the mansion of a multi-millionaire scumbag who made his money from a creepy brand that exploited young women. You remember *Girls Gone Wild*? It was a disgusting semi-pornographic DVD series where JOE FRANCIS— yes, that's him—and his film crew filmed/exploited a bunch of naive, intoxicated college girls and got them to show their tits (and more) on camera. They would then sell these videos to fucking gross old men. It was nearly impossible to watch TV in the late 1990s and NOT see the *Girls Gone Wild* infomercials full of drunk eighteen-year-olds in Cancún being manipulated into shaking their asses for the camera. Yup . . . that guy. I was seventeen years old and new to L.A., so . . . he seemed nice? I met him out one night and he invited me to lunch the next day, which seemed harmless enough. It's lunch! Daylight = safe, right?!

The next day he and his driver picked me up in a Bentley. I felt so fucking cool, even though he was on his phone the ENTIRE way talking to none other than . . . Andy Dick. How do I know it was Andy Dick on the other end? Oh, I got into the car, he nodded smugly at me, covered his Razr phone, and whispered, "Gimme one sec, sweetie [he had already forgotten my name], I'm on with *Andy Dick*." He completely ignored me the entire drive FOR ANDY DICK.

We went to a Mexican restaurant where he REMAINED ON THE PHONE WITH ANDY DICK. The waiter approached and I thought, for sure, he'll hang up now. NOPE. "Hold on, Andy Dick," he said and proceeded to order some shrimp tacos. He then whispered to me, "Get anything you want, babe." AND THEN HE CONTINUED TALKING THROUGH THE ENTIRE MEAL TO ANDY DICK. But I was hungry, so I brushed it off. I was a canned-corn-in-my-apartment gal getting free top-shelf margaritas, enchiladas, and guac.

After lunch, Joe finally made eye contact and spoke. "Sorry about that, Lauren. I was on with Andy Dick. But you're kinda sexy and deserve better treatment. Want me to give you a tour of my *massive* house?"

Being the young and naive idiot I was, I agreed. After all, it was DAYTIME.

He gave me a tour of his mansion, which was truly impressive to a midwestern teenager who grew up thinking luxury is shag carpets. He had photos on the walls that showed him posing with presidents and rappers. While I was staring at the one of him and Bill Clinton he must have disappeared because suddenly I heard him yelling, "Hey! I'm up here! Let me show you the upstairs."

Oh, cool. The tour continues! So even though this was playing out like an after-school special about date rape, I went up the stairs because, remember, it was DAYTIME.

I walked up the marble staircase and down a hall with about fifteen doors. When I got to the sixth door I heard him say, "Come in." And just like the naive heroine of our after-school special, I went in.

And here's the reason I was too scared to tell this story in my first book: When I walked in, he was on the bed completely naked with his dick in his hand. And very casually, he goes: "Hey."

I ran as fast as I could along the hallway and down winding stairs out to his Bentley. I was terrified and out of breath, but when I asked the driver to please take me home NOW AS FAST AS POSSIBLE, he didn't even look fazed.

You're thinking there cannot POSSIBLY be more unwanted dick stories, RIGHT?! That would be RI-DICK-U-LOUS, right? (My trauma puns are therapeutic, okay?)

AND YOU'RE WRONG! THERE'S MORE UNASKED-FOR DICKS!

When it comes to unwanted dick sagas, I RULE. It's not a title anyone wants, Queen of the Unwanted Dicks. There's no tiara, and look before you sit on that throne. But you know what? I survived, and I'm here to tell you about ALL THE UNSOUGHT DICKS, so let's continue . . .

When Colleen and I were in our early twenties, we went to

many over-the-top, lavish, and oh-so-sleazy Hollywood parties. Any young, even slightly pretty girl could get herself invited. Even if you weren't invited, you could probably flirt your way inside. At one of these fancy-douchebag parties we met a jolly old Frenchman who said he was big in the fashion industry. Within five minutes of meeting him, he invited us to fly across the country to Miami the next day. Instead of seeing the bright *rouge* flags (that's RED in French—thanks, Ms. Toussaint), I excitedly exclaimed, "Hell yeah! This is not sketchy *at all*! Bon voyage, bitches!"

Colleen looked at me skeptically for a quick minute, then realized I was going to go, with or without her. "Alright," she said begrudgingly. We were broke and I wanted to experience life and see the world, and this rich *monsieur* (who if he was in fashion was no doubt inspired by his desire to surround himself with barely legal models) was generously offering. Colleen and I would be together and we had each other's backs, so it would be *totally* safe, right? Right?!!

The next day, we hopped on a plane with the decrepit French dude and his perpetually stuffy nose. After we landed, he took us to his Miami penthouse. It looked like he bought it in cash from Tony Montana. It was pure *Scarface*. As soon as we walked inside, he pulled out a bag of very pure Colombian cocaine. So I knew, at that moment . . .

We'd made a great decision!

Cocaine was my drug of choice and this shit was *undiluted*.

It didn't take long for Mr. Fashion to try to get into our tube skirts. I remember him patting his thighs, gesturing for me to sit on his lap, like the handsy uncle at a family reunion. I had just snorted a massive line of coke and was too numb to care. As I sat down he began aggressively bouncing me up and down while singing an unfamiliar song in French. I turned to Colleen, my eyes wide with panic, and she looked back at me. Have you ever attempted to lock eyes while being bounced like a child on the knee of a dirty old degenerate? We needed to escape. See, we had assumed he'd flown us first class across the country to his penthouse and given us unlimited drugs just out of the kindness of his definitely failing heart! But now there seemed to be some kind of . . . expectation? I excused myself from his lap and went into an extravagant restroom. My sister followed. Colleen and I had a secret meeting amid the gold-plated and fully mirrored decor. I remember looking at an infinite number of Colleens reflected on the ceilings, walls, and floors. My face was now deliciously numb.

"We have to get out of here," I said, grinding my teeth. "It's only going to get worse."

"How the fuck do you suppose we get back to L.A., Laura? I'm out of money and you never had any."

My sister had been supporting us with her hard-earned waitressing money and I was always too high to get a job. Our funds were running out fast. So while Monsieur Perv was busy cutting up lines, we sneakily gathered up our bags, nicked a bottle of Dom Pérignon Rosé, and bounced. We sprinted out through the swanky golden doors while that overripe hunk of cheese was too snowed up to notice. We ended up at a cool hotel bar near the beach and met some cute younger guys. We told them about our situation and they told us we could stay with them. *Phew* . . . right?

RIGHT?!

Actually, they were very cool (well, most of them). We were having a great time, when one of the guys, let's call him Jason, confided in me that he had terminal cancer and was dying. He said they had found a brain tumor and he was given only two months to live. This was his last trip out with his best friends, and then he was going to fly back home to spend his last month with his nine-year-old daughter. My heart was breaking for this poor man and his poor daughter. I was bawling and comforting him as best I could. I just kept telling him how sorry I was. How unfair this was. He started sobbing with me. We held each other. He told me he needed a minute alone in his hotel room to cool off, and I was welcome to come. "Of course," I said through my empathetic, alcoholic tears. My sister was flirting with one of the cute guys by the bar and didn't notice I had left. BUT IT WAS FINE.

Up in his hotel room, Jason pulled out his phone and showed me several pictures of his beautiful young daughter. He was weeping hysterically, "My little Stacy is going to grow up without her daddy."

I answered with a guttural sob. I was bawling uncontrollably, the most heinous ugly cry you've ever seen. Two months left on this earth?!

"It's not fair!" I wailed, imagining how I would feel as a young child if my father were dying. "IT'S JUST NOT FAIR!!!" I was sitting on his hotel bed, looking at a photo of Stacy and him together, father and daughter. They looked so happy. My face was now bright red and puffy from tears and vodka. I was incredibly distraught, and I continued mourning the inevitably near death of this man I'd just met. As I turned to console him with a hug, I noticed through blurry tears that he was now completely naked. His limp penis was just hanging there and I was so rattled by the fact that this man was dying, I couldn't really comprehend what was happening. I had been so busy falling apart over this now completely naked man's impending death to comprehend his slowly impending penis. At that VERY moment, Colleen called my cell phone looking for me. She sounded frantic!

"Laura, where are you?!"

I could barely speak through the tears. "I'm . . . I'm . . . up . . . I'm upstairs with—wait, what's your name?" I asked.

"Jason," he said quickly, dong still on full display.

"I'm with Jason and, oh my God, IT'S NOT FAIR!!!! It's tragic. The world is fucked! We're all doomed, ESPECIALLY JASON!"

"Laura, spit it out! What is going on?! Where! Are! You?!!!" Colleen was freaked out.

"JASON'S DYING, COLLEEN! HE'S DYING!"

"Right this second?!"

"No, but in two months! And Stacy will be all alone!!! Without a daddy! OH GOD, PLEASE HEAL THIS MAN!!! Also . . . I think his dick is out?"

My sister yelled back in her sternest teacher's voice, "COME DOWN HERE NOW!"

When she used that tone, I always listened. I turned to Jason, who sat beside me casually, holding his weird-looking dick in his hand like a corn dog. I was still too distraught (and too fucked up) to acknowledge his intentions. Honestly, in my mind, he was too sad about dying to even know his dick was out. This wasn't sexual assault, it was GRIEF. It made sense at the time. I looked deep into his bloodshot, vacant eyes, which signaled not sexual predation, but rather a profound sadness.

"I have to go, Jason," I said. "You are so, so strong. SO strong. YOU CAN BEAT THIS."

"I'm definitely going to *beat this*," he replied, still gripping his ghastly cock.

I found Colleen back at the bar and told her everything about how Jason only had sixty days—TOPS!—to live. As I recounted the story, things finally started to click . . .

"All of a sudden, he was . . . naked? And sitting next to me on the bed. But . . . but . . . Wait. Hold on a damn minute . . ."

Colleen and I looked at each other, our eyes widening. This couldn't be! How could anyone . . . ?! But I almost fell for it. I CRIED for this guy. Just to make sure, Colleen and I approached his friends and asked if Jason was dying from cancer. His friends looked at us in shock. "Huh? Jason? He just finished running a 5K race . . . He does not have cancer."

Still in denial, I chimed in, "Well, maybe he does and he just didn't want to tell you guys! Maybe he wasn't ready to tell you!"

"He's healthier than all of us. We've grown up with Jason and if he were sick, we'd know. He definitely, one hundred percent does not have cancer."

"What about his daughter, Stacy?"

"Jason doesn't have kids."

Now I was beside myself, and who was that girl in the photo?! I get saying you're six feet tall on a dating app to get replies, or claiming you're an astronaut to get some moon pie, or pretending you have been celibate for a year waiting for the perfect girl to come along, or should I say cum along. It's *all* shitty, BUT THE CANCER CARD?!! That's an *all-time low*.

Jason's friends were embarrassed for him, AS THEY SHOULD BE. They kept apologizing to us, profusely, about what Jason had done. Anyway, Colleen actually stayed in touch with one of Jason's friends after that trip, and once a year we'd text him and ask if Jason was still kicking.

"Yup," his friend would text back. "He just ran the 10K this year. He's healthier than ever." We continued asking if Jason was dead yet for about four years straight, and unfortunately he never was. What a piece of shit! Colleen and I still laugh (and cringe) about it to this day.

And if you're wondering how we got home, we convinced *another* group of guys we met later that night to buy us tickets—and they did! And we never saw Jason or that horny French grandpa again.

There is one last story that I was too scared to tell, but not because someone was masturbating over my face. In this one, *I* was the guilty party. As guilty as the desperate clowns I just told you about? No, but still. What I did wasn't illegal (*or was it?*) or evil (*well, maybe a little?*), but it was humiliating.

As an eighteen-year-old girl from the Chicago suburbs, I wasn't used to seeing famous people unless you count Judy Hsu, our local news anchor. Los Angeles is crawling with celebrities, though, from A-list Oscar winners to I-know-that-guy-from-somewhere celebs like GHB Jared. So I was dancing at this club one night, and I locked eyes with a HOT and extremely well-known actor on a show that, at the time, was a major hit. I'll call him . . . Ryan. He kept staring at me (I swear!), and so I decided to play it cool and say something extremely chill and seductive. Something like:

"Why are you staring at me?"

I was only eighteen, but I had MOVES.

"I wasn't," Ryan said.

"Yeah, whatever," I shot back as I tossed my drink and sipped my hair *at the same time*. Literally, my hair got caught in my mouth and I drank it along with my shot, and it was disgusting. I told you I had moves. I never said they were good moves.

I committed fully to playing the bitchy, hard-to-get girl. And it fucking worked. I turned my back on Ryan and ignored him. A few excruciating minutes later, he walked up to me. I tried to act aloof, like I was used to being approached by hot celebrities all the time and this was no big deal.

"Hey," he said.

"Yeah?"

"Maybe I *was* staring," Ryan said.

"I know," I said, just like Angelina Jolie probably would have.

"You're pretty," he said. "Let's hang out."

We danced, drank, and flirted the rest of the night. I knew my cool, aloof-girl act was over when he asked me to come back to his apartment and I blurted, "Say no more!"

This time, instead of being assaulted in a mansion at lunchtime after eating enchiladas, I had a super sweet and fun hookup that was totally mutual. What a revelation! Ryan did everything right—but as for me? In this story, I am the asshole.

After he fell asleep, I stared at him in bed for a while with my face about two inches from his face. I was not being creepy—he was famous, okay? He was on the biggest network show in the world at that time—oh, and also he was the lead character. (Are you guessing? Googling? Both?! Hint: It aired between the years 2003 and 2007. THAT'S ALL I'LL SAY.) I stared because I had to imprint his features in my brain so I would remember them forever. As I stared, I thought, *Dude. I am in bed with a gorgeous, kind celebrity.* I just knew my friends would never believe me unless I had proof. Actual, tangible proof. I knew cutting off a lock of his hair wouldn't work, and my janky-ass phone didn't have a camera. This was 2005. We had flip phones and an ancient relic called a BlackBerry, which had no camera. I quietly got out of bed and started scanning the room for some hard evidence to show my Downers Grove besties, because those bitches would demand proof.

And there it was. Just sitting there on his dresser: his wallet. And inside his wallet, his driver's license.

I looked back at Ryan still passed out from last night's vodka sodas, and then I looked at his wallet. My eyes ping-ponged back and forth as I contemplated doing the unthinkable . . .

My interior monologue went: "My friends will never believe me unless I have proof. *But stealing is wrong, LAURA!* You just gave him your sweet, sweet poontang! The least he can do is let you take his driver's license to make you seem cooler to your high school friends. *Don't do it, Laura.* Do it, Laura. Do it. DO IT NOW. IT'S THE HOTTEST SHOW ON TV! AND YOU SMASHED THE LEAD CHARACTER. DO IT NOW OR YOU'LL REGRET IT FOR THE REST OF YOUR FLIP-PHONE-USING LIFE" (in 2005, we thought flip phones were the end of the road for technology).

I grabbed his wallet, took out his ID, and ran out the front door.

WHO. DOES. THIS?! This was among the most shameful acts I've ever committed, which is saying A LOT.

For the next six months, pulling out Ryan's license and telling my story became my go-to party trick. It was endlessly funny and I felt endlessly cool. My friends loved it, strangers loved it, I loved it. My friends and I even hung the license over a piano in my apartment at one point, like it was our most prized family photo. I never heard from Ryan again after that night, probably because he realized I was a psycho who stole his license and he had the wisdom to avoid me for the rest of his life. I did see him a few years later, though. I was really drunk (imagine!), so it's a little fuzzy, but I said something smooth like, "Hey! Do you remember me? We had *horizontal refreshments* together, if you know what I mean."

He stared at me blankly. I didn't even really know what I was saying, so how could he? I continued: "You caught me in your friendly fire, remember? I baked your potato? You bisected my triangle?"

He nodded like he was starting to remember our lovely night years ago. I kept talking—I shouldn't have, but I did. I should have stopped while I was, maybe not ahead exactly, but at least not where I was HEADED.

"Your driver's license must have fallen into my purse that night we hooked up, or else maybe you gave it to me to keep by accident? Anyway, it was so weird that I ended up with it—I have no idea how that happened! How're you?!"

His face went from intrigued to horrified. I could see the wheels spinning in his beautiful ocean (hint, hint) eyes. I had just told on myself—and I would have gotten away with everything if I had just shut up! Impulse control must be nice. He probably thought he had misplaced the license that night because we were so intoxicated, AND I RUINED EVERYTHING!

Ryan looked at me like *I know exactly what you fucking did, you psychopath, and if you don't step away I'm calling the police.* I now say without ego (well, maybe a little) that today, years later, I'm weirdly more famous than Ryan is, at least on social media—and even so, if someone stole my license and hung it over their piano *I would be honored.* But I also understand that what I did was completely unacceptable: I caused a perfectly nice person an unnecessary trip to the DMV. And that is just low, vile, and shameful—not #MeToo low, but VERY close.

CHAPTER 7

Am I Doing This Right?

When I was a kid, there weren't labels like Helicopter or Free Range or Snowplow Parent. At least not that I was aware of. If I *had* to classify my parents, though, I would probably describe their style as . . . Lots-of-Fun-Often-Drunk-Well-Intentioned-Also-Chaotic Parenting? Is that an official category? Let's say it is.

Sure, there were times when we could barely pay the bills, but my brilliantly creative mom, Marilyn, always made sure we were rich in fun. She was one of those extraordinary women who always felt they were destined to be a mother. Marilyn made it her primary purpose to devote her days to making sure we were happy, warm, fed, entertained, always learning, staying creative, and having a fucking blast. Every single Halloween, she would HAND-MAKE our costumes (she sewed her own wedding dress, so believe the woman's got talent) and tell us the most riveting ghost stories around the fire . . . She would go the extra mile by blindfolding us all while passing around a bucket full of "body parts" to correlate with the horror story . . . peeled grapes for eyes, spaghetti and red sauce for organs. We'd each warily dip our tiny hands in the bucket full of "human remains" in horrified delight. It was disgusting, spine-chilling, and we had an absolute BALL.

We never had the money for Disneyland season passes or family trips to Paris; it was more like "let's stay home and play with random shit laying around the house"–type fun. One day my mom came up with a game called "bubble gum wars" where we literally just chucked bubble gum at each other for *hours*. It was so much fun for absolutely no reason. I had a bucket of Bazooka paper-wrapped pink bubble gum. You know, the kind that tasted like Pepto-Bismol? And my sisters each had their own bucket. Then we went in the front yard and just chucked the shit out of them at each other until the sun went down. I can't remember if there were specific rules or guidelines to this made-up game or if we just whipped shitty gum at each other for no reason. Apologies to any suburban wildlife that got stuck reading those crappy comics on the inside wrappers.

We didn't have rigid schedules or many rules thrown at us, just: 1) Be nice to people. 2) Don't die. 3) Never trust a woman with big hair. That was basically it. What we did have were plenty of wild adventures. Our house was full of an unlimited supply of sugary foods, which attracted all the kids on the block. My mom also always cooked portions big enough to feed the whole neighborhood . . . and we often did. Anyone and everyone was welcome at our house. Our mom always had arts-and-crafts activities ready for us, whether we were attempting origami or designing friendship bracelets or making magazine collages of all our favorite things. She is a brilliant storyteller and would always encourage us to tell stories as well. We would sit around for *hours* at a time and connect through stories. She also had music *blasting* whenever she would attempt to clean our beautifully chaotic home: Tom Petty, Joni Mitchell, and Neil Young on rotation. We had no clue what bedtime was, and sometimes there was so much clutter in our rooms we could barely find our actual beds—*but* at least we knew how to spray the shit out of each other with the garden hose while doing endless backflips on our massive trampoline with NO NET. Or stay up way too late planning our early retirement from the valuable Beanie Baby collection we'd acquired—the signature bear that mom got for five dollars was now worth two hundred! We were set! When there was a torrential downpour, my mom didn't tell us to come inside and dry off, she told us to go outside and bounce around, get dirty, pelt some mud at each other. The downside was that because our bedrooms could become so disarrayed, my friends weren't even allowed upstairs most times. I think my mom was afraid someone would get buried under a pile of Pixy Sticks, Slinkies, Bop Its, Furbies, and old shoes, never to be seen again. If only she knew how grateful we kids were to have such an utterly devoted, brilliantly creative, ingeniously crafty, and endlessly loving mother. And that having a sometimes-disorganized house is not a moral failing. Some brains—especially creative ADHD ones—struggle with things like organization more than others. Plus my dad was never home, not even on the weekends, so she had three young kids (plus every other kid in the neighborhood) to look after and no help. Some of my friends' moms were super strict, structured, and obsessed with their kids eating healthy, and having a spotless house. Whereas my mother was more focused on us having as many card games, chocolate chip pancakes, and belly laughs as we possibly could. There are upsides to both, but let's be honest . . . I GOT THE BETTER DEAL.

The house was surely riotous, but there was so much love. Our parents never discouraged us from doing what made us happy (and for me, that was missing school and being a clown). They encouraged us to find who it was we were and own that. I think that might be why I felt like I could grow up and become successful at acting. No one had ever said, "Laura, stop doing that Australian accent and calling your overalls 'dungarees' and go do your algebra homework!" They didn't discourage me from making horror movies in the backyard—in fact, my mom *helped* me make fake blood for the final massacre scene. I think that kind of support and love is the secret sauce when it comes to parenting kids who grow up to believe they can do anything or be anyone. My mom might not have properly cleaned the carpets for sixteen years, but she loved and emboldened us with everything she had.

When my mother wasn't putting all her time and attention into us, she was tutoring kids with learning disabilities in our living room. She would charge the families next to nothing for her services because she just loved to do it. Sometimes she would do it for free if she could see the family was struggling. It didn't matter that we could barely pay the mortgage. Money was unimportant to her, sometimes to a fault. Once a month, she would drag me out of bed at four thirty in the morning to feed the homeless at the local church. I resisted, but she made sure my sisters and I went. This was one area where she *was* militant. She made sure we learned the importance of helping others in need. Though we kicked and screamed to stay in bed each time, we always felt so good afterward—grateful for our cluttered beds and baskets of bubble gum.

My mother is actually with us in L.A. as I'm writing this. I can hear my supportive mama downstairs right now, singing "The Ants Go Marching One by One" to my two sweet babies. Once again saving the day so I can finish writing this book. She's just always been there. Always.

When it comes to my parenting style, as much as I loved my wild childhood, the jubilant chaos that I grew up with doesn't really work for us today. Maybe because I'm balancing work and momming, I need a reliable routine. I need structure. And to know where things are. Stephen and I try to focus on a style that I guess could be called Structured-but-Not-Too-Structured-Because-We-Both-Have-ADHD-and-Can-Never-Find-the-Pacifier Parenting. It's a struggle. We try our best to have consistent schedules and routines for our kids, without being *too* rigid. They are free to get dirty and play in the rain, but also dinner is at 5 p.m. so come inside! And perhaps we will net our trampoline.

When Alfie was six months old or so, we still had no schedule in place and I was anxious as hell. Everything was intuitive and it was stressing me the fuck out. If I thought he was tired, I would rock him or nurse him to sleep. If he looked hungry, I'd feed him. It sounds crazy to even write this, but that was how my mom parented, by instinct alone. Not having order and routine worked well for Mom, but not for me. I remember most days I'd spend nearly TWO HOURS trying to get the boy to nap and when he'd *finally* clonk, it'd be for a whopping twenty minutes!!! This was *not* working. Something needed to change. I had a nanny friend come over for a day and create a very specific routine that I believe is magic:

7 a.m.: Wake up!

7:05 a.m.: Breastmilk!

8 a.m.: Cereal and banana!

9 a.m.: Nap!

11 a.m.: More breastmilk!

11:30 p.m.: Play/tummy time!

12 p.m.: Solid lunch!

1 p.m.: Nap again!

3 p.m.: Titty milk!

4:30 p.m.: Half-hour cat nap!

5 p.m.: Solid dinner!

5:15 p.m.: Take a walk!

6 p.m.: Bath!

6:30 p.m.: Drink from the milk wagons!

7–7:30 p.m.: BED!!!!

This. Changed. My. Life! Now, we aren't *super* rigid with it and as we know, shit happens! (Literally. So much poo.) But overall, having this posted on our kitchen cabinet to refer to was life-changing. "Oh! This is why Penelope is inconsolable . . . it's time for her cat nap!" And BOOM, she's out . . . It's wondrous. My mom hadn't taught me about schedules because she just knew *roughly* when a baby was tired or hungry or needed a walk or more tummy time, but I sometimes struggled with it. For me, it's a balance of intuition and routine. If Poppy is under the weather, of course I will do more breastfeeding and an earlier bedtime. If we decide to have a weekend outing, well, fuck the entire routine altogether—let's do this! Okay, we haven't really done that. We are the definition of homebodies and we are happy with that. Stephen and I are in *absolute* awe of our friends who are determined not to let their young kids ruin their social lives and ability to travel. They're always going on these crazy trips with their small kids and it's truly remarkable to see. Planes, rental cars, hotels, and restaurants with toddlers and babies sounds like my idea of purgatory. Like, FUCK that. But also, bravo! We are genuinely impressed with your impressive feat—one that we are nowhere near mastering.

Of course, the schedules and our children are forever growing and changing and just when I think I've got it all figured out, they have the audacity to keep evolving. I think overall I am getting the hang of being a mother, but for some reason there is always that one older white woman online, most likely named Nancy or Barbara, who loves to try and tear me a new one. She'll DM me that Alfie's hair is too long "for a boy" or tell me to dress my baby in "real clothes" and not pajamas. But I'm sorry, is my baby going to give a TED Talk today? Maybe one day, yes, but not now, Barbara. *This* day he will not require a tuxedo.

Just like the Boibs brand was inspired by a Nancy who scolded me for breastfeeding in public, the PJs All Day line became a thing because of the Barbara who told me to dress up my perpetually napping, unemployed baby. When I posted her comments online, SO many mothers said that they have faced judgment around this as well. Mostly from old-school mothers-in-law, but nonetheless, I can't stand it when anyone mom-shames, especially *other* moms. Shortly after Barbara attempted to shame me for dressing Alfie in onesies, the sometimes enormously petty me thought, *Let's make onesies with "PJS ALL DAY" written on them. HOW WOULD YOU LIKE THAT, BARB?* I posted the idea on social media for feedback on the design and I was met with a *storm* of envious moms:

"Screw our babies, I WANT PJS ALL DAY! MAKE THEM FOR US!"

"YEAH! FUCK THOSE BABIES. WE WANT TO BE COMFORTABLE TOO!"

"YEAH! MY ADORABLE LITTLE LIFE-RUINER HAS ENOUGH ONESIES! WE WANT TO WEAR PJS ALL DAY TOO!"

"YEAH! I'M SICK OF FUCKIN' JEANS! LET'S BURN OUR JEANS AND WEAR PJS ALL DAY! MAKE SOME COMFY-ASS JOGGERS SO I CAN FUCKIN' BREATHE!"

The moms had spoken loud and clear. They were craving comfort and we delivered. We created a super-comfy sweat suit line with PJS ALL DAY written on the hoodies, joggers, and oversized tees. Then right as we launched them . . . a global pandemic hit. Everyone was on lockdown, no one was leaving the house, and everyone just wanted to be cozy in this uncertain time. Jeans were officially a thing of the past. So THANK YOU, Nancy, for your mom-shaming comment, because it inspired me to create a line of comfy-ass clothing at a time when we needed it most.

Nancys have also tried to take us down for helping feed our two-year-old oatmeal with a spoon because "he's old enough to feed himself!" I've been criticized for feeding my kids plant-based food as well, even though I'm hypervigilant about making sure they get all their nutrients. YES, INCLUDING PROTEIN. I've been rebuked for keeping the tap running too long when giving my newborn a relaxing sink bath: "Turn the faucet off! How wasteful! We're in a drought!" Excuse me, am I a golf course owner, generously drenching my massive courses with sprinklers for the amusement of rich ass-holes? No, I am a mom giving her wee tiny newborn person a WEE

TINY SHOWER in the wee tiny sink. DO YOU NOT SHOWER, NANCY? I bet your big-girl showers use way more water than my wee tiny sink ones do. If California experiences a water shortage, I highly doubt it will be traced back to Penelope Marilyn Hilton's wee tiny sink baths.

There are plenty of "momfluencers" out there who claim to have all the answers—how to raise sustainable babies, how to teach your infant Mandarin in three days—but I am not one of them. I don't have the answers, mainly because what works for me and my children may not work for you. I just want what's best for them, as most sane parents do. I continue to learn as I go and do my best on this wild, exhausting, ever-changing, totally incredible ride called motherhood. I also love asking *other* moms how to do something. Maybe it's the youngest child syndrome . . . Being the baby, I never think twice about asking how the fuck to do things. I actually view my incredible followers like encouraging friends/older sisters. And a lot of times, y'all are RIGHT. Like the commenter who told us that we shouldn't put Alfie's car seat front-facing yet. That was a HUGE wake-up call. Once he grew to twenty pounds we turned it forward-facing, but we quickly learned, from you, that it was not the safest option. We turned it back around and made an educational vlog about the importance of car seat safety. I also love to ask you about your favorite products. It's incredible because we can all look at the most liked suggestion, and that one is usually the best! You amazing women are helping me so much, so THANK YOU! Sure, there will always be Nancys and Barbaras and Karens, and maybe that's not all bad . . . they do keep inspiring me to create amazing shit! I've also come to realize that there are many more inherently *good* people in the world than there are judgy assholes.

Because of my past and Stephen's, of course we worry about our kids and addiction, yet I know we have only so much control. Our therapist told us we should have the conversation with Alfie and Poppy about drugs and alcohol when they're between eight and ten years old, since there is so much addiction in both our families. He said to explain in a child-friendly way that if they drink or use, it will likely not end well.

And how should we think about gender, whatever the fuck that is? When I found out the sex of each of my kids, I had dramatically different reactions. When I was pregnant with my first, Stephen and I were visiting my sister Colleen and her husband, Greg. I was twelve weeks along and the doctor was going to call us with the sex of the baby. At the time, I decided it would be cute if the doctor told Greg first, and then Greg would dress their daughters, Madeline and Eleanor, in either pink dresses if it was a girl or blue dresses for a boy. Which, honestly, was NOT very woke of me—BUT! at least we weren't blowing up fireworks and burning down an entire forest!

Stephen kept saying it was a boy, but I was convinced it was a girl. My mom had three girls, my sister Colleen had two girls, and my sister Tracy also had two girls. How could I NOT have a girl? It was fate. Now, I truthfully didn't care either way and just assumed that our family produces humans with vaginas, so I was SURE of it. But then the night before the big reveal, I had literally THREE dreams that I was having a boy. I mean crazy-vivid dreams where I would be sitting and waiting in the Victorian living room from 1837 to find out the sex, and my two nieces would dance into the dimly lit room wearing flowy blue dresses, their undeniably blue fabric swirling around, undoubtedly telling me that *it was a boy*. I woke up from the first dream around 1 a.m. and I remember saying to myself, "Huh, that was weird, but it was just a dream and dreams mean absolutely nothing . . . right?" I went back to sleep and had the SAME dream *again* . . . then BOOM, I woke again. This time it was at 4 a.m. For a split second I was convinced it was real. But no, just another nonsensical dream. *I'm definitely having a girl. That's what we have. We have girls.* Back to bed I went, and sure enough . . . I had a THIRD DREAM telling me that I was having a person with a penis! It was like my baby's soul was trying to communicate with mine. He was trying to tell me and every time I doubted it, he was like, "Why aren't you listening to me? Do we really have to do this *again*, Mom?" After the third dream, when I awoke in the morning I told Stephen immediately, "I think . . . I think we are having a boy. I was SO sure it was a girl just yesterday, but these dreams . . . they were so vivid and happening all through the night." He responded with utter assurance, "That's because we *are* having a boy. I know it." Anyway, I know it's not cool to care about your baby's gender, and truthfully I see why. It doesn't matter at the end of the day. I mean, it *shouldn't* matter.

The next frosty morning at the farmhouse, Stephen and I were chatting with my mom in the kitchen, while Colleen was strumming her favorite Serge Gainsbourg song, "Di Doo Dah," in French on her Viennese guitar from 1850. Meanwhile the kids were playing outside on the massive tree stump and Greg was on hour six of manually grinding organic peaberry coffee beans from Tanzania, when my phone rang. It was the doctor!

Greg grabbed the phone from me and chatted with the doctor. What had I done?! I can't believe I let him be the first to know! He then quickly rounded up my two beautiful toddler nieces, Eleanor and Madeline, and took them to change. The rest of the family and

I waited anxiously around the wood-burning fireplace. I couldn't tell if I was shaking from nerves or mild hypothermia.

We had our eyes closed for what seemed like an eternity, then we heard the words "YOU CAN OPEN NOW!" When we opened our eyes, there they were, dancing in blue. Stephen and I held each other and sobbed. I was still sort of shocked coming from a family of all girls, but I didn't care either way! We were just so elated to be growing our family.

When I found out that Penelope was a girl, my reaction was completely different. There was no dramatic reveal, no gender party. But when the nurse called to tell us, Stephen filmed my reaction.

"So, do you want to know the sex?" the nurse asked.

"Yes," I said.

"It's a girl!"

In the video I look stunned, which I was. Stephen then ecstatically cried out, "Oh my God!" and hugged me hard. We held each other, our hearts beating fast. Then Stephen exclaimed through joyful tears, "How do you look after a girl?! How does it work?! Can I wrestle with her?!" We laughed. "Of course you can," I said. "Just . . . gently."

Instead of feeling over-the-moon like any sane expecting mother, I was instantly filled with shock, excitement, and—dare I say it—angst. It sounds horrible to say out loud, so Penelope, if you're reading this in the distant future . . . I love you, let me explain, and don't ever do cocaine. I always said I would be happy regardless of the sex, and I was! But my body had this immediate, uneasy, panicky reaction, this intense fear that . . . *she would be like me*. Would she also have to take geometry three times? Would she get arrested more than once and be nicknamed "Cuffs" just like her mom? Have an abortion at fifteen? Would she, like me, have a slew of unwanted dicks thrown in her face? Would she date Damons and Jakes and Brians? Would she one day get so high she thinks the pizza delivery guy knocking at the door is a serial-killing rapist? With her DNA, the grim possibilities were endless.

I just remember having this deep fear and thinking, *What if I can't protect her?* And I didn't have that with Alfie. Am I sexist? Misogynist? What is wrong with me? Then, once the intrusive thoughts left my pregnant queasy body, I suddenly felt a wave of hope. In that moment, I became determined to do everything in my power to make sure she wouldn't experience the level of trauma that I had. I would be stricter than my parents were with me, but not so strict that she would rebel. I would not drink or use in the home the way my father had. We would have a sober, always safe home. I would teach her about her sexuality instead of pretending it didn't exist. I would make her feel that it is okay to tell me anything and everything and that it's always a safe space in our home. I would encourage therapy, even if she feels okay, because talking about your feelings is never a bad idea. My daughter will be safe, loved, protected, and encouraged. Her father will be sober, kind, and encouraging—and she will know she deserves these things for herself.

My father is a complicated man: incredibly smart, funny, and kind when sober. He's also stunningly beautiful, like a cross between John Travolta and Jeff Buckley. Unfortunately, alcoholism runs deep on that side of the family and my daddy caught it. When he drinks too much, he can get mean, especially to me. He would make fun of my big feet, knowing that I had a deep insecurity around them, or just say cruel things that cut deep. I'm not resentful, because I know he is sick and that acting like a drunk dickhead is just a symptom of his disease. One night, we were driving home from a family dinner at a local Japanese restaurant. It was the kind of restaurant where the chef cooks everything on the table right in front of you, flipping sizzling shrimp and mushrooms right onto your plate. We did this only a few times a year since it was expensive, so this dinner was a BIG deal for the family. On the ride home, I told my dad how happy I was that he had met Mom and that it was meant to be—because then they made me. I was feeling happy and I wanted to share a sweet moment with my dad. Instead of saying something sweet or kind, he laughed maniacally and said, "Do you really think my purpose in life was to have *YOU*? Get out of here!"

Now admittedly, it seems a bit self-involved that I thought the reason my parents met was to make me, but *I was a child*. Now, I think about that night and imagine one of my children saying those things. Would I laugh in their face and tear them down? No way!

"Of course, my beautiful Penelope, of course we were meant to make you. YOU and your perfect feet are the light of our lives."

"Uh, Mom, why are you bringing my feet into this? That was a little out of left field."

"I'll explain one day."

This is undoubtedly what I would say. Once I shifted my mindset from fear to love, I started to see things clearer. Maybe I was broken at one time, but I've pulled myself out, sobered myself up, and am now living a life beyond my wildest dreams. My daughter will see me dealing with my problems, not drinking to mask them. She will see me doing what I love for a living, knowing that anything is possible. She will see what a (mostly) healthy relationship looks like.

After the initial fear of hearing I was having a girl, of course I was elated. I remind myself (sometimes throughout the day) not to think about what could go *wrong*, but rather what could go *right*. *Stay in today, Laura, stay in today*. Stephen and I are determined to do everything in our power to help our kids stay healthy and safe and be who they were meant to be. Maybe we'll be a little stricter than my parents were with me and a little less strict than Stephen's parents were with him. (As did most kids in 1970s England, he got many "clips 'round the ear.")

I try to parent with as much empathy, respect, boundaries, and understanding as possible—and it's progress, not perfection. No spanking or yelling, and rather than instilling fear and punishment, I'm much more drawn to using positivity and patience. I'm NOT saying it's easy all the time, but it's what feels right to me. I NEVER want my children to feel scared of me or Stephen. Alfie is approaching two and a half as I write this and is having some epic meltdowns from time to time. Rather than punish him for not being able to control his emotions, I want to make a safe space for him, try to understand, and have empathy for what he is going through. I think there's a misconception that "gentle parenting" means you just let your child get away with murder, but that's not how I see it. I think instilling routine, boundaries, and rules are vital to guiding a happy, well-balanced kid. BUT WHAT THE HELL DO I KNOW?! Not much, bitch! But I'm learning more every day.

End of the day, I just want my kids to be whatever and whoever they want to be. I don't care what pronouns they use or who they want to marry (just nobody named Damon, please). I want them to go outside and play freeze-tag in the rain and express themselves however feels right. If they want to be an artist, great, but if they want to be a tax accountant, also great!

This is a book about marriage and motherhood and milk and

MISTAKES—the good, the bad, and the WTF-is-she-thinking-giving-her-toddler-son-a-man-bun? I LIKE Alfie's bun! But if you must know, his hair didn't get long because I have some sort of compunction against cutting it. His hair got long because Alfie vehemently said "no!" The kid didn't want a haircut, okay? I choose my battles—and his long, curly locks are GOALS and you know it!

CHAPTER 8

Come Inside My Brain

*O*KAY! TODAY *is going to be a PRODUCTIVE DAY! YES MA'AM! I'm filled with energy and creativity!!! Just going to take a quick morning walk . . . Make a mental gratitude list . . . Visualize my goals and affirm that I am NOT in fact a lazy piece of shit. I am not a lazy piece of shit. I am not a lazy piece of shit. Gotta get my brain cells fired up. But not too fired up in case they flame out and die young . . . Can that happen? Must google that now . . . Turns out abnormal neuronal firing can occur, leading to death of brain cells. Oh, great. It's time to start writing . . . but first coffee . . . hold on . . . Where are the coffee mugs? Like, really? Where have they ALL gone?! Who is hiding them? I bet they're all scattered over Stephen's fucking studio. Why did I marry a crazy man who hoards cups? Okay, I suppose I'll use our two-year-old's sippy cup. Triple-shot cappuccino with oat milk and off to work I go . . . Wait, is the latest that coffee is good or bad for you? I can't remember! Must google it . . . Okay, turns out if you drink coffee* *you will definitely 100 percent not get Alzheimer's because it increases the production of granulocyte-colony stimulating factor, whatever the hell that is . . . But wait, this other article says that too much caffeine can shrink the brain and cause dementia . . . WTF? What was I supposed to be doing and why am I now standing in my bedroom? How did I get here? I have to pee. Was that Alfie crying or Poppy? Why do I have my phone in my hand? Should I watch some TikToks? No, Laura, you have a lot of work to get done. Speaking of getting work done: Kylie Jenner. I should probably google her right now. Thaaat's an entire new face. Wait . . . How did two hours just go by?*

Welcome to a day in the life of my brain, ladies and gentlemen— the brain of a woman who was diagnosed with attention deficit hyperactivity disorder at the tender age of thirty-four! I'm sure none of you are surprised by my diagnosis after seeing my completely chaotic videos . . . BUT I WAS! My entire life, I NEVER knew what was happening in my brain, medically speaking. I just thought I was a wildly inattentive, dangerously impulsive scatterbrain who loved to cause trouble and who hated authority of any kind. I thought that EVERYONE spent hours looking for their eyeglasses while they'd been perched on top of their head the entire time. I thought it was NORMAL to forget how you got into the shower or to get distracted by a funny bird during a funeral. Doesn't everyone start cleaning the bathroom and then remember they forgot to floss and then remember they're due for a dental cleaning and then grab their phone to make an appointment but then open TikTok instead and then get inspired to write a comedy sketch about crooked teeth? That's NORMAL, right? Apparently not!

But you know what? I am grateful for my beautifully fucked-up brain. Neurodivergent brains are the best brains, in my opinion (maybe I'm biased because my entire family is neurodiverse). My brain is wrinkly in places it technically shouldn't be, according to my brain scan. But still, I would not have it any other way. Even my shitty memory is a blessing. It keeps me present (a huge plus when there are many things I'd rather not remember). I chose to focus on the unique strengths that come along with ADHD, not just its challenges. I am highly creative, a great conversationalist, spontaneous, and courageous . . . all character traits highly associated with people with ADHD. Yeah, it's a pain not to remember why I walked into my living room and sometimes it's incredibly irritating to be driven by dopamine and craving stimulation all the fucking time, but I personally love being neurodivergent and get along with neurodivergent people the most. I like the freaks, the eccentrics, the off-the-wall, peculiar types (I even married one). We often have an unusual way of seeing the world, and I believe it's *oftentimes* a gift. My beautifully imperfect brain has gotten me to where I am today, and I am eternally grateful for it. But of course it has caused some major struggles . . .

Growing up, I *hated* school. As you can imagine now that you've peeked inside my mind, I could not focus for the life of me. I could focus on making people laugh and getting myself into trouble, but that's it. All those years in school, I had no idea that I had this "disorder." My mom thought I was perfect just the way I was (thanks, Mom) and my dad did not believe that ADHD was real. Or any mental health disorder, for that matter. The man doesn't even believe in eyeglasses. "You've just got to exercise your weakling eyes!" he says, then he blinks aggressively a few times as proof of concept.

I tried so hard in school, but it was a constant struggle. I was also deeply obsessed with making the other kids laugh. Sometimes

I would just walk into a classroom and people would laugh. I'm not sure if that's a testament to how powerful my gift was, or how mean kids can be about tall, gangly girls? Either way, I killed! My primary goal became MUST MAKE PEOPLE HOWL, and I followed that impulse until it became my whole career.

Humor was in part a defense mechanism to hide the fact that I was SO horrendously bad at school. I literally took one Scantron test BACKWARDS AND UPSIDE DOWN without even realizing it! When I was finally diagnosed with ADHD last year, I called my mom and asked, "Did you really not know there was something going on, since I got straight Ds and I was constantly in detention?"

She replied, "I just thought you didn't like school and you liked to socialize, and that's who you were and I didn't want to change that." I respect my mom for that, in a way. If I'd been medicated, would I be writing this book? Okay, probably yes and a LOT faster. Would I have met Stephen and had our babies and made people laugh online and created Helen Horbath if my mind had been "calmed down"? I suppose I'll never really know either way. My mom did feel guilty after I got my diagnosis, but like my guru Anne said, "I wouldn't be who I am today, I know that for sure." I don't define myself by ADHD, although it's made a whole lotta things make sense for me, and I wouldn't have it any other way. Have what any other way? No idea!

According to my psychiatrist, my brain is a 6.5 on a scale of one to ten. If you're super competitive, you might think a 6.5 is tipping toward failure, but with my history I'll take it! I'm used to getting Ds. I trust my doctor because if he's good enough to examine Miley Cyrus's brain, he's definitely good enough to probe mine. I do wonder what her score was. Was her brain bumpier than mine? Prettier? More curvy or svelte? Was it hornier? Smarter? Was it better at puzzles? Since I have no impulse control, if I ever see Miley in person I will probably ask her all these questions and more. Miley, if you're reading this, let's get a green juice and compare brain scans.

I went out to Costa Mesa during summer 2020 to meet with the psychiatrist and get the results of all the tests and scans I had done, but I had no idea what to expect. I'd initially gone because I was worried about my memory. The scan he did is called a SPECT study (single-photon emission computed tomography) and I have no clue what any of that means, but I believe in it with my whole heart. It has something to do with gamma rays, which is 100 percent a sign from Gamma Alice (rest in power)!

So instead of asking how you're feeling, this doctor examines the brain and uses a neuroscience approach. His method made sense to me (sort of) and he explained things in a way that clicked (a little). Like, one reason I have intrusive thoughts specifically at night might be that growing up, my sometimes unpredictable, alcoholic father was more erratic at night. So perhaps I'm subconsciously craving that adrenaline rush. I DON'T FUCKIN' KNOW, MAN. During that visit, when he told me I had ADHD, I told him that I did not want Adderall. I did not want any drugs. My fucked-up brain was working for me (sometimes). Of course, if I became so depressed I couldn't get out of bed and wanted to kill myself, I would take medication. If I was not functioning and present for my husband and kids, I would take it. I'm not against it when necessary—I just know myself and I don't want to change anything or risk getting hooked on anything if I don't *absolutely* need it (LOL, WHO *AM* I?!). I want to learn from the pain and the hard things, even though it is not easy. If it ever gets so hard that I can't function, I will take what the doctor prescribes.

Mental health issues run deep in my family. My uncle Don, who was also my godfather, always said he was meant to die at the age of fifty-three. That's when his father (my grandfather) died. Also, my uncle Don's brother and best friend, John, died at fifty-three. My psychiatrist would have loved Don's brain, because the man was an encyclopedia. He could quote any film or book, word for word. His memory was impeccable, unlike mine, but he didn't really have any friends or a wife or kids, and he lived with his mom, and then with *my* mom, his entire adult life.

My favorite chocolates are Fannie Mae Pixies. "Fanny" means vagina in Australia and the U.K., which has nothing to do with anything but it's still hilarious. Another fun fact: My mom's first job was working at the Fannie Mae factory in Chicago. Every time I saw Uncle Don, he had a box of Fannie Mae Pixies for me and my sisters. Since he was just as sweet as the chocolates he'd give us, I used to ask him, "Uncle Don, how come you don't have a girlfriend or boyfriend?" And he would always answer, "Why would anyone date me?"

"Because you're funny, can quote *Bye Bye Birdie* word for word, and you always bring us chocolates. You're a catch," I would reply. He never believed me, though.

When my grandmother passed away and her house was sold, Uncle Don had nowhere to go. My mom took him in and he moved into my sister Tracy's old room. Whenever my sister Colleen and I would fly home to visit, he would still have boxes of Pixies for us at the airport. He got increasingly reclusive over the years and continued to call himself a loser. He had a part-time job at Target for a while, but as his mental health got worse he would lock himself in Tracy's room for hours on end. My old room was next to his, and once I heard him playing porn loudly—and I was so disturbed I slammed my door so he would know I'd heard him. I slept downstairs on the couch after that.

Eventually, Uncle Don stopped buying us Pixies or helping my parents with bills or food or chores. My mom was upset about it, so I told her to confront him. She had a bad knee and she was outside shoveling snow because my dad was working, while Uncle Don had locked himself in Tracy's room.

"You're right, I'll say something," my mom finally agreed.

About a week later, my mom called me, in tears.

"Don is missing," she said.

"What do you mean?"

"He never came home from work and it has been two days," she said. "I told him he needed to start contributing if he was going to live here, and he stormed upstairs and then left."

"He'll be back, Mom," I said. "Try not to worry."

The next day, I got another call from my mom. This time she was hysterical.

"He's dead, Laura. Uncle Don is dead."

"What? No! How?!"

"Two detectives showed up at our doorstep this morning," my mom said. "A maid found him in the bathtub of a Holiday Inn. He slit his wrists. There was no note. Just his laptop opened up on the desk with one word typed on the center of the screen . . . '*Euthanasia.*'"

Uncle Don, my godfather, was fifty-three.

My mom tried so many times to get Uncle Don to seek help, but he never did. Maybe it was because of shame or fear or both. Maybe if he'd gotten help, tried medication or therapy or both, he would still be here. Over half of young adults in the U.S. with depression don't get help for it. Why? Maybe by talking about it and taking the shame out of it, more people will be inclined to reach out for help.

One of my favorite cousins, Marie, struggled a lot too—just like me. She was my dad's brother's daughter, and she was four years older than me. We were close growing up. She *loved* to do my hair and makeup every Christmas Eve. I would arrive at the family party looking like a typical six-year-old child, but after Marie was through with me I looked like those scary beauty pageant kids. My parents were horrified, but I was in heaven! She always made me feel so beautiful and glamorous and I just adored being around her. I pretty much idolized her.

One Christmas when I was about twelve, we went to the movie theater to see *Austin Powers: The Spy Who Shagged Me* (a classic, and I stand by that!). Anyway, that Christmas Eve, she introduced me to weed for the first time. I remember at first saying, "I'm not a druggie, thanks!" But Marie, so beautiful and charming, convinced me that I was making a big mistake. So I took a hit. It was a terrifying experience, and I couldn't wait to do it again. Marie was gorgeous, creative, and incredibly compassionate. She even refused to eat meat as a kid (and later as an adult) because she cared so deeply for animals. When you grow up in Chicago, that's saying A LOT. Chicago is the "Sausage Capital of the United States" and people there are *very serious* about their meat. Anyway, Marie was a perfect blend of warmhearted and shamelessly raunchy. I guess it runs in the family. She was effortlessly alluring, her bold nature was magnetic—all the boys wanted her and the girls wanted to be her. She was a Clery, though, so eventually we both lived up to our lineage and became addicts. Marie and I would go out drinking in Chicago together, before I knew that it was a problem. Back then, I just thought we were having a good time (which we were). When I went to L.A. and ultimately got sober, Marie unfortunately continued drinking and using. As you probably know, addiction is a fatally progressive disease; she got into pills, then coke, and then heroin. She went through several rehabs and husbands. She also had an adorable eight-year-old son who hung on her every word.

Over the years I would get calls and texts from Marie, *always* from new numbers since she was constantly losing her phones or not paying her bills. Once, she called me from a motel room where she was shooting up while her son hid in the closet. She said she couldn't bear for him to see her like that, yet she just couldn't stop. I *begged* her to go to rehab, but at that time she was too scared of Child Protective Services taking away her son. She loved him more than the world, but not more than drugs. She was just so sick. That's the thing so many people don't understand about addiction. It's an illness, like cancer or diabetes. I was no better than Marie, but she was just so consumed by her addiction and for whatever reason, she could not stop. She went to jail multiple times and had a long record, so she couldn't get work. At one point, she asked me to tell her story on my social media for millions to see. She manically pitched it as *the life of a super-hot yet totally misunderstood felon*. She thought it might help her get a job. I was actually open to the idea, but like many of her other grandiose plans it eventually fell comatose. She desperately wanted a second (and third, and fourth, and fifth) chance at life but could just never seem to stay clean. It broke my heart each time she slipped, because I *knew* her potential and how incredibly kind and brilliant she was underneath her illness.

She would call me sometimes hyping herself up, talking about how great things were going and asking me to give her advice on her latest million-dollar business idea. Then the next call she would say she felt worthless and that she couldn't stop using and was afraid she was going to die. It went on this way for years and I never once judged her for it, because HOW COULD I? Every time we spoke it was for hours, and she would tell me the craziest stories about her chaotic drug- and toxic-romance-filled life. We would end up crying together and then laughing hysterically moments later. I know addiction is not funny, but we had a very dark sense of humor and we had to laugh at our illness or we would go MADDER than we already were. She would send me pics of her looking stunning in this super-elegant dress with perfect hair and makeup, and then I'd look down and notice her ankle monitor.

The last time I saw Marie was in Chicago at my baby shower when I was pregnant with Alfie. I barely recognized her because she was so skinny—she was just not in good shape at all. It was a hard thing to see. But somehow, she was still her sweet, sassy self. When she got to the baby shower, she *loudly* started telling everyone in a super-dramatic tone that she barely made it because she was in the emergency room with her third husband all night. Apparently, he "fell off a ladder while he was painting at four in the morning and a broken wineglass stabbed him in the neck, needing sixty-eight stitches!"

Then she proceeded to show *everyone* photos of husband #6's mangled, bloody neck as they awkwardly nibbled their adorably decorated cupcakes.

Welcome to a Clery baby shower, bitches!

When Marie left, some of my family was like, "She one hundred percent stabbed him."

"No way! Definitely not," I said. "She doesn't even eat meat, you guys." But they were convinced. IF she did it, and that's a huge *if*, I bet you it was self-defense.

The last time I ever spoke with Marie, she called me super excited—perhaps *unnaturally* exhilarated, if you know what I mean. Regardless, there was undeniable joy in her voice when she told me she was six months sober, so I chose to believe that. She said she had gone to treatment and while she was there, she fell madly in love (shocker) with this hot twenty-three-year-old and was four months pregnant with his baby. She was ecstatic to be having a second child. Marie had recently moved to Florida with her young new fiancé and her sweet eight-year-old son. She was trying to get away from some local bad influences who were using heroin heavily. (I mean, *Florida* to escape *drugs?* Come on, Marie!) She then told me she had a super-exciting new business venture and that I was the first person she would tell about it. I don't know for sure if this was true, but she sure loved to make me feel special. She made me feel like her best friend every time we spoke. She told me that she knew I had never judged her and so she always felt safe telling me her deepest desires.

"Okay, bitch, you ready to hear it?!"

"Spit it out, Marie!"

"Pregnant porn."

"Sorry, what?"

"I want to be a porn star and I'm pregnant. So, pregnant porn! Laura, I know I would kill this!" Normally I would tell her that might not be the best idea, but for some reason in that moment I just surrendered to all of it. It had been so many years of crazy, chaotic stories about jail, guns, drugs, and ankle monitors. I decided just to love and support her in that moment.

"Marie, I think you'd be *great* at pregnant porn," I said.

After about an hour of laughing, we got off the phone. Within thirty seconds, she sent me the last text I would ever receive from her. Well, it was more like a novel:

After all this crazy shit passes, you and Steven and Alfie NEED to come back to the farm and ride horses with me!! It was so much fun when we all did that so many years ago as kids. I also wanted to tell you that after our chat it was so easy to make my decision. I know that if I put in the time and effort necessary, I will not only love my job, but I will be successful. Quite possibly very successful eventually. Even though there are an incredible number of models who are much hotter than me and have perfect bodies, those things only go so far. I have a natural gift of being able to connect on a very personal level with most anyone almost instantaneously. Because they can tell that I genuinely care. And I'm fun, flirty, candid and quite often I'm pretty funny . . . Not even close to your level of funny but when I'm on a roll, I'm on a really good roll . . . Plus I'm still pretty hot for 37, my tits and ass look better than ever and I am the biggest freak when it comes to sex and trying new things. I don't fake anything . . . quite the opposite. I've been told by MANY guys that I've been with that I was the most fun, freaky, sexy, passionate, and addictive woman they have ever been with. And they weren't just trying to get in my pants—they had already been deep inside them 😛 . And trust me, I never compliment myself. I'm actually really, really hard on myself but I'm working on it. I guess I'm telling you all this because you are literally the FIRST person I have discussed this with. I'm not sure if you know how it feels to keep something locked away in your mind (for a year and a half now). Something that you are actually SUPER excited about. And you just want to tell someone, but for some stupid reason or another you don't. I'm just lucky to have someone like you who I feel comfortable opening up to about anything. I wish I had talked to you about it sooner. So again, sorry for the long text, but it feels great to be able to write to you about it. I definitely don't expect a reply since time is super precious. Ok, thank you SO much again for always being there and never judging. Love ya tons!!!! 💋

Exactly two months later, Marie had another relapse, overdosed in the shower, and she was gone. She was six months pregnant. And just two weeks after she passed, I found out that I was pregnant for the second time too.

One night I was alone in bed and it was pitch black in my bedroom. I was sobbing as I thought about Marie. I was so devastated that she never made it out and I was furious with myself for not texting her back. I read her last text to me after our long call and then was so distracted by my children and my life, I never fucking texted her back. Then, just two months later, she was gone. I was bawling like a baby as I reminisced about all the times we'd spent together, from little happy kids to full-grown addicts. All the times she had told me she never felt good enough and that she was *convinced* everyone had given up on her. I thought about the time she kicked her living room window until it shattered, then grabbed a shard of glass and stabbed herself in the neck, while both her parents watched in horror. (Neck stabbing was clearly her thing.) She was screaming for help, desperate for unconditional love and acceptance. Yet, she herself was incapable of accepting it. I just wanted her to know that she was *always* good enough. Even as a kid, she was always trying to lose weight and be perfect . . . I wished she'd known she always was. I wondered if maybe she was finally at peace. And then, at that very moment, the lights in my bathroom flickered. It was her! It was a sign. She was telling me that she's not suffering anymore! It was so clear. I cried even harder, and then I actually smiled because I heard her voice *so* clearly at that moment:

"Bitch!! I'm chillin' up here, it's amazing!!! I feel great, and I love you so much!!! You're killing it out there, Laura!! I see you, girl! Oh and by the way, I did try to murder my husband because he pushed me down the stairs and called me a worthless slut. It *was* self-defense. Nonetheless, thanks for defending me at the baby shower!! You've always had my back!!"

She laughed hysterically and so did I. I could FEEL her presence so strongly with me.

"Alright, I'm gonna go shoot some ghost porn, which is a thing. Later!! Love ya tons!!!"

Laughing through my tears, I said, "I love you too, Marie. Talk soon."

CHAPTER 9

I'm Rich, Bitch!

Because I grew up rich in *imagination*—and poor in everything else—it is not lost on me that at this point in life, I am extraordinarily blessed. I have a successful career that I love. I have a home and am building a dream home down the road. I have a nanny five days a week so I can work, and I can buy the good coffee at Whole Foods.

Growing up, I never bought into the idea that I needed tons of money to be happy. Despite the occasional dysfunction in my house, I would say my childhood was pretty rich in love and creativity and toys from the discount store. I think that where I'm from, it was just culturally common to hate on, blame, or demonize "the rich." I even remember my parents doing it. Almost like if you had money, you MUST be greedy and evil.

My parents tried to shelter me from the fact that we were always one missed payment away from foreclosure. I had my basic needs met, so I never really felt poor. My mom would go to discount stores and wrap everything up nice, so we had tons of presents during the holidays. I think she did this because she herself grew up very poor and as a kid, she always wished she had more presents to open. She did everything to make us feel spoiled and loved. We got to unwrap so much stuff it was like we were the Rockefellers, even if it was just slippers and toys from Dollar Tree. Whatever else I needed, I stole. It was a system that worked out great for me, and my parents never knew. Or if they did, they ignored it because they were probably relieved that I had a new pair of "free" jeans.

My shoplifting started when I was about fourteen years old and lasted until I was about seventeen, when I pulled a massive heist and stole some scar cream from a CVS. (I had tried to speed-shave my happy trail and it went very wrong. I *needed* that scar cream.) I always justified my stealing by bragging that I would *never* steal from your grandma or a family-owned store or a fruit stand on the side of the road. I would only steal from the big corporations because: fuck them! They were probably immoral and they were most likely the bad guys. I was stealing from THE MAN, whoever he was. I couldn't afford makeup or cool clothes otherwise, but I also loved the risk of it all. I told myself I was an edgy suburban revolutionary who just happened to need some Bonne Bell eye shadow.

In my house growing up, the story was always the same: We don't have enough money, we're broke, the end. These days I feel lucky that I can afford to help out my parents when they need it. When my mom was a tutor for kids with learning disabilities, she would charge thirty dollars an hour, while our neighbor Sue Anne did the same job and charged over one hundred dollars an hour. Whenever I questioned my mom about it and asked why she didn't rip off these rich private school families like Sue Anne did, she would say, "I'm doing it to help the kids, not for the money."

That's noble for sure. But if my mom had been just a *teensy* bit greedier, could I have walked into the store and simply paid for my low-rise stretchy flared jeans?

My mom grew up one of eight siblings who shared ONE BATH-ROOM. Her father died very young and her mom was a teacher, so they were poor. My dad grew up middle class; his dad owned a food packaging company. I think my dad was in over his head when he was tapped to take over the company—it was too much for him. He loves building machines and he's brilliant at it, but *running* the entire company made him crazier than he already was. It would do okay one year, and then horribly the next, and he was always taking out additional mortgages. One year he did well and we took a family trip to Disney World in Florida, which was a *huge* deal for us. Despite that one trip, we were never really rich in money or possessions—but we were as happy as any loving, wildly dysfunctional American family can be.

I read about a study that found prioritizing money actually makes people less happy in their lives, and I BELIEVE IT. Once we equate money with happiness, we're never really satisfied. We always want more, instead of being happy with what we have. What's actually improved my happiness is having meaningful relationships, a sense of community, and focusing on how I can serve, through my work, as a mom, as a wife . . . okay, and also being able to order groceries straight to my door. That is fucking awesome. Weirdly, when I wake up in the morning and ask, "What can I give?" I'm often much happier than when I ask, "What can I get?" Ironically, I believe this mindset is how I've managed to succeed to the degree that I have! It seems that the more you give, the more you *get*!

When I moved to Los Angeles for the summer at seventeen, I slept on a friend's couch and constantly begged my sister Colleen for money. By the time I turned twenty-two, I was a full-time, working actress, but I was working *just* enough to cover my bills. Between jobs I would file for unemployment, and that eight hundred dollars a week would hold me over until the next job I booked. I couldn't believe how much money I was getting! My attitude at that time was: All I need is *just enough* to pay rent and eat food—and buy drugs, obviously. I don't need money to be happy, I would tell myself. I'm an artist and so long as I have a rented roof over my head and some things to eat and snort, I'm good! What I didn't realize was that by adopting that mindset, I was affirming that all I wanted was *just enough* to get by . . . And what do you know? I'd always earn *just enough* to get by.

Then I started reading about the law of attraction (don't judge me!) and positive affirmations (seriously, stop!). After a bit of cringing, it clicked. I started believing that our *thoughts* can actually help create our reality and we are more than just the products of our environment. I started understanding that we are more powerful than we think and are actually the co-creators of our lives. It was a *huge* revelation for me and I became *obsessed* with learning more about it. Because I had been affirming *just enough*, that's exactly what I was getting. My entire life, I had been affirming that "I don't need money. Money is for greedy people. Rich people are ALL bad." But that's complete bullshit! Because think about all the GOOD one can do in the world with a lot of money. How many lives you can help. I totally reframed how I looked at wealth and realized I needed to feel *deserving* of it—that was key. Once I realized that my poverty mindset—the mindset I grew up with, "there is never enough money and that's the way it is"—was not serving me, I made the conscious decision to change my thoughts. I needed to start affirming abundance in ALL areas of my life: happiness, relationships, health, creativity, wealth, work, philanthropy.

The Secret may be the cheesiest movie and book of all time, but I think the ideas are something worth looking into. It explains (with melodramatic music) the idea of using the Law of Attraction to create your dream life. Quantum physics and vibrations aside, the Law of Attraction works for me because it keeps me focused on what I DO want rather than what I DON'T want, making it easier to achieve my goals. (EASIER, not effortless!) Practicing the Law of Attraction has helped me to rewire my subconscious mind from a fear-driven poverty mindset to a loving and abundant one. Suddenly, my goals became more attainable. My life got bigger. A lot of people think it's hippie-dippy spiritual New Age bullshit, but all I know is that this hippie-dippy bullshit *works* for me.

Before I started doing all of this reeducation, I assumed that wanting more meant I was greedy. I would be a sellout who wasn't acting for the love of my craft, but for a paycheck, and that's not me—I'm not that asshole! I had adopted my parents' outlook about money: There would never be enough, so I would never work for money but *for passion*. If I could just keep up those eight-hundred-dollar unemployment checks between filming Burger King commercials and failed TV pilots, I'd be fine. But then I suddenly realized: Why *not* have more? Why. Not. Me?

I definitely did not want to be greedy, but I did want more out of life than an unemployment check and a bathroom in which I could not fully stand up. It was incredibly hard at first to reprogram my mind and BELIEVE that we live in an abundant world and ANYTHING is possible. But with consistency and a dash of delusion, I got there. ASK AND YOU SHALL RECEIVE, I would say to myself eight thousand times per day. Believing I was deserving of more than the bare minimum took doing countless abundance meditations and visualizations every morning and every night. The more money I made, I reasoned, the more I could give back! Also, I wanted a nice fucking house! Yeah, I did! I don't think there's anything wrong with that. And I wanted to actually BUY those overpriced jeans this time! I did not want Alfie and Poppy visiting me in the clink just because I couldn't free myself from a scarcity mindset.

So, I started saying daily affirmations and believing that I could achieve anything I wanted. Something I learned early on is to start every visualization with a gratitude list. This is KEY . . . Before visualizing what I wanted, I had to become incredibly grateful for what I already had. The sun! Eyes for seeing! My sobriety! My kids! Trees! A mouth to taste with! A butthole to wink! Only when I acquired a state of gratitude could I begin affirming the goals I wanted to achieve: a healthier body, meaningful relationships, a beautiful home to raise our family in, a plant-based food bank that would feed millions in need. I learned how important it is to affirm and visualize the goal *as if I had already achieved it*. After my gratitude list, I would start out by saying several times a day: "I am so happy and grateful that I'm making millions of people laugh around the world and making millions of dollars doing it." It felt weird to say it at first . . . until it didn't. Why NOT me?

I've read about NBA players visualizing the ball swooshing through the hoop before the shot. Or, the Wright brothers visualizing a plane—and now we can sit eating peanuts in a metal tube hurtling across the sky. I always say my goals in the present tense, like they're already happening. I don't say, "I hope to have an animal sanctuary one day." I say, "I am so happy and grateful that I have an animal sanctuary—my family, the animals, and I love it so much." I say it as if it's happening—and then it often *does*. Delusion is the key!

Maybe the reason so many people have been unsuccessful with manifesting is because they don't realize that EVERYTHING we say is an affirmation, positive OR negative. So if we have sixty complaining, fearful thoughts (negative affirmations) where we focus on what we DON'T want, and only five positive affirmations where we focus on what we DO want, which side wins?

I am not a magician, but I can tell you that changing my own mindset and outlook on life—from fear to love, from scarcity to abundance—has helped me achieve my dreams in ways I never could have imagined. It also took hard work and dedication, but most important was that I believed it was possible and that I felt deserving of it. It's also really fun, you guys! Who doesn't want to get grateful for the things they have and visualize awesome shit? TRY IT! If *I* can successfully retrain my bumpy-ass brain to believe anything is possible, SO CAN YOU. Once I started regularly affirming, "I am making millions of people laugh on a consistent basis and making millions of dollars doing it," I started having incredibly viral comedy videos and made a huge monetary jump! My mom chalks it up to hard work and talent, but I call shenanigans! I know PLENTY of comedians and actors who are way more talented, funnier, and/or prettier than I am, but who can't seem to catch a break. I've even tried promoting them on my platforms, but still they fall back into the struggle. I don't think it's their fault—just like me, they were conditioned to believe that life is not fair, there's never enough, and that struggle is just the way it is. But I've learned that it really doesn't have to be! We CAN defy the odds. We are deserving of happiness and abundance in all areas: relationships, money, love, health, mind-blowing orgasms . . . We are *all* deserving of these things!

I forced Stephen to listen to these super-cringy YouTube videos of positive affirmations with me. At first he was like, "Laura . . . this is creepy." I was like, "I know, NOW DO IT!" You can visualize your ideal job or house or relationship or dog or peacock farm . . . Don't hold back. Create your dream life in your mind. Years later, Stephen and I STILL do this every morning on our walks, and every night before bed. It has been LIFE-CHANGING. "I'm happy and grateful we continue to stay sober! I am happy and grateful we are in perfect health, physically, mentally, and spiritually! I am happy and grateful our kids are creative and healthy and thriving! I am happy and grateful my pelvic floor muscles are stronger than Wonder Woman's." THE LIST GOES ON. It's powerful stuff.

It'll feel phony at times, like when you're in a shitty-ass mood and you need coffee and you're scowling and grumbling, "I'm so happy and grateful . . . ," but just keep doing it. Note that I'm not preaching "toxic positivity," where you ignore the problems in your life. I'm a big proponent of working through problems and then MOVING THE FUCK ON—getting back to focusing on what we DO want rather than what we don't.

Stephen dropped out of school when he was fifteen years old and he still can't read music, yet he ended up working on some of the world's biggest films, including *Moulin Rouge!*, *Transformers*, *Madagascar*, *Mission Impossible*, *Ocean's Eleven*, *Ocean's Twelve*, and my personal favorite, *Zoolander*. His mom and dad met while working as ushers at a movie theater. Despite the fact that he didn't come from money, somewhere within him he believed he could do this crazy thing and become successful at music. I had that same drive and belief. I think part of it is having parents who encourage you, instead of saying things like, "Well, you know acting and music are pipe dreams." Because both of our parents never told us we couldn't, we believed we could. And so we did! I always figured, *why not me* when it came to pursuing my craft, and Stephen always believed the same. Now I apply that mindset not just to my career but to every area of my life.

Obviously, that does not mean we just sat on the couch and visualized ourselves successful. We each worked for years to get to where we are now. We also had no Plan B. No backup plan. It was either this or simply *pass away*. But like I said, I know MANY people who are smarter, prettier, and funnier than me and they can't seem to catch a break.

I got my first real paycheck as a teenage server at Dolly's Cafe in Downers Grove. I was horrible at the job, spilling coffee on people and never remembering which table ordered what. That job lasted about a week, but I remember the tips I did manage to make felt exciting at the time. Before that, I never imagined that I could be independent because I had no idea how to take care of myself. If they taught us anything about finances or saving money or earning a living in high school, I was probably too stoned to listen. During my early twenties, I was 100 percent convinced that I needed someone else (usually a guy) to take care of me. I felt truly incapable. I told myself I could live off boyfriends and friends and family because I needed to focus on my craft, which at the time was doing tons of drugs and some occasional acting. That was my big plan: live off other people and do tons of drugs until the world recognized that I deserved to be the next Kristen Wiig.

It didn't work out, you guys.

When I dated Rudolf, the patient and practical German, he told me I needed to get a "*ficken* job." It's weird that he wasn't satisfied with a girlfriend who laid in bed all day smoking weed and eating potato chips, but everyone has their issues. I ended up getting a job as a server at a members-only cigar bar in Beverly Hills, so I guess I had put my week at Dolly's Cafe behind me. Big surprise—I was terrible at the job, but somehow it lasted nearly a year. Or maybe it was five months that felt like a year. Once I spilled a drink on Alec Baldwin!

The girls that worked at that cigar bar were all beautiful, and they expertly flirted with the customers so they would make bigger tips. I don't know how they did it—they seemed so effortless and there I was, freakishly tall, awkward, and doing my best not to spill red wine on George Lopez's Armani suit. After five months on the job, I decided I could not go on. I just wanted to do what I loved, making people laugh—and not with physical comedy involving drink orders spilled on crotches. I woke up one morning and just didn't go in. Instead, I got stoned and ate chips on the couch. Eventually, my manager called.

"Hello?"

"Um, Laura?"

"Yep."

"Are you coming into work?"

"Nope."

"Well, you have to. We need you here."

"I actually *don't* have to," I said like a legal scholar.

"Then, you're fired?"

"Yes, I'm fired," I said.

"Thanks a lot, Laura."

"No problem!"

We hung up, and I booked a TV pilot the very next week!

Now, I am not suggesting you just up and quit your job tomorrow like a crazy person—I am just telling you my story, as a crazy person.

Lady Gaga, Oprah, AND Will Smith believe in the Law of Attraction . . . so it MUST be true, right?! Oh, and before he was famous, Jim Carrey wrote himself a ten-million-dollar check for "acting services rendered" and he carried it around in his wallet for years. I'm not denying it requires a tremendous amount of talent and perseverance to "make it," but I strongly believe those are only part of the total equation . . . Jim set his path by writing that check and believing it was possible—and then it was! Doing these affirmations can be fun—it's like a game of Delusional Projections, which is a board game I just made up and am ready to license!

Stephen and I often lie in bed marveling at all the things we have manifested thus far. It's never an "if" for us but a "when." My current favorite affirmation is, "I am so happy and grateful that we continue to heal the world through our gifts." I strongly believe that we all have God-given gifts and if we use them for good, each and every one of us can help to heal this world. When we stand in our purpose, it is incredibly gratifying and energizing, and our lives become richer in every way. I know I sound like Tony Robbins with a twat right now, but I LOVE THIS SHIT!

You know what else can be magical? Masturbation! On my quest to move through my postpartum depression after having my second child, one of the self-care acts I committed to was regular "*ménage à moi*" sessions. I was completely determined to quash the simply untrue thoughts I had of being undesirable, unattractive, and broken. I was ready to stop beating myself up and start rubbing myself down. I was DONE crying over my perceived "broken" vagina, bloated belly, and overall negative outlook on, well, everything. I was ready to get my self-confidence back and remind myself that I was still just as—if not more—sexy, smart, and worthy as I was before having children. So, there came the brilliant idea of Self-Care Sunday . . . every day. And I must say, visiting my safety deposit box more frequently has truly lifted my spirit *and* my pelvic floor.

This very morning in the shower as I was "scrolling my mouse wheel" I had the idea to visualize what I wanted to achieve physically, mentally, and spiritually. I know it seems strange not to fantasize whatever is the weird sexual fad of the moment, but I decided to instead visualize my body in perfect health! I visualized having an even MORE loving and joyful relationship with Stephen, and having the strongest, wettest, most magical whisker biscuit ever. I visualized world peace for all and having a healthy, loving, fulfilling, meaningful life, and then . . . I came.

Now, before you look at me like I'm crazier than you already thought I was, HEAR ME OUT! Female masturbation is incredibly good for you (I say female because men usually need less convincing). Women are often selfless to a fault, and they probably say they don't have the time or even the desire, for that matter. But I challenge you! Yes, you! Take just ten minutes today to paddle your pink canoe and visualize a beautiful life. Just being in the moment with it is absolutely wonderful and loaded with benefits like stress reduction, better sleep, better sex, better moods, and even more energy. But manifesting your life desires during OR directly after the act makes so much sense to me and has been a deeply powerful experience. Here's why I think it's a million-dollar idea: Masturbation increases your feel-good chemicals and when you FEEL good, your vibrations are HIGHER. When your vibrations are higher, it's easier to manifest the life you desire! Once you're flooded with feel-good chemicals, visualize the life you want! So yes, I am suggesting that you raise your vibrations with your vibrator.

Science will never *not* be confusing as shit to me, but the quantum theory of physics sort of makes sense. It explains that everything is energy waves. When our energy is vibrating at a lower frequency we feel like punching ourselves in the face, but when we are vibrating at a HIGH frequency we feel like dancing on a rooftop to Cyndi Lauper! When we engage in positive, healthy behaviors and thoughts, we are raising our vibration and attracting the fucking amazing into our lives! I'm choosing to believe in this theory because it's fun and "Girls Just Wanna Have Fun." Also, isn't it easier to focus on what we *want* rather than what we *don't want* when we're loaded up with feel-good chemicals? YES, BITCH, IT IS! Are you with me?! COME ON, GIRLS!!! Actually just COME, girls!

Yet another random article I read on the internet tells us that we are using only 10 percent of our brains, and as a mom even that is a stretch. WHAT IS THE OTHER 90 PERCENT DOING?! Napping? Sometimes I wonder what would happen if we utilized the other 90 percent. How can we put it to work to help create a better, more peaceful world? One of my greatest teachers is a woman named Louise Hay. If you haven't heard of her, I urge you to look into her, watch her videos, and read her books. The woman is absolutely brilliant. She passed away peacefully in her eighties and I feel compelled to help her ideas live on. Louise dedicated herself to teaching people how to live a positive and empowered life, but what I love most about her is that she didn't really find herself until she was in her forties. That's when her life really began.

When Louise was young, her teacher told her that she was "too tall to dance," and she held that self-limiting belief for most of her life. Then, at seventy years old, she signed up for a dance class. She was determined to learn. She's just incredibly inspiring and teaches that it is truly never too late to find your joy and create the life you've always wanted. She rightfully preached that the totality of possibilities is awaiting us! Her brilliantly cheesy YouTube videos taught me to ask myself regularly, "What am I doing with my mind to break barriers? Am I willing to let go of my limitations and walk through my fears? Am I willing to love and accept myself exactly as I am? Am I willing to love and accept others for exactly who they are? Am I willing to forgive? How far am I willing to go to expand the horizons of my thinking? How often do I go beyond my present limits? DO I stop at 'I can't' or do I say to myself, 'MAYBE this time I CAN'?"

Perhaps there is always a way so long as we are open to it. One of the things I want desperately for everyone on this planet is to feel unconditional LOVE and safety and JOY.

For years before I got sober, I was a selfish, self-seeking, fear-driven asshole with an unrelenting drug problem. As much as I hate to admit it, becoming less selfish did not come naturally to me. I had to work at it. I had to force myself in the beginning to get up in AA meetings, walk over to a newly sober person, and say, "Hey, I'm here if you need me," even though I really couldn't think of anything worse. Actually, if I think about it, being of service IS selfish in a way, because it feels so fucking good. Like I've said before, I truly believe that the more you give, the more you get. So yeah, I guess I'm still selfish but in a new, better way. I also believe I had a spiritual awakening as a result of getting sober and working the Twelve Steps. And for me, that looked like a continual shift in perception from fear into love, a deep desire to be good, to do the right thing, to not steal the driver's license, or drug the sister, and generally to keep my side of the street clean. Also to help others in any way I could: helping others get sober, helping others laugh through my comedy, helping others feel less alone through vulnerability, helping Stephen make sandwiches. Every morning I pray to a god I still don't understand, "God, please keep me sober today. Remove my fear, replace it with faith, and help me to serve in whatever way you see fit."

Of course as you know, I'm still batshit crazy sometimes, struggle mentally, and SHIT HAPPENS . . . but I am now able to at least recognize my insane thoughts. I'm able to walk through my fear and sadness (sometimes quickly, sometimes slowly), and I'm able to continue affirming that I have come to this planet to learn to love myself and share that love with those around me. It can be really hard, in trying times, to say cringe shit like that . . . but I want to be happy! So I will CONTINUE to be a cheeseball and affirm that *all is well in my world, everything is working out for my highest good, and I am safe.* And the bad times seemingly fade away because I refuse to hold on to them for too long. I refuse to believe that we were brought onto this earth to live in a perpetual state of suffering. I CHOOSE to forgive myself and others to set myself free. I CHOOSE to trust the process of my life. I CHOOSE to begin my day with gratitude. And I ATTEMPT to balance my life between love, work, and play. When I walk through the day thinking ONLY about what I can gain, it's oftentimes unfulfilling and anxiety-inducing. But when I think of the good I can create in the world, whether it's being a present, fun mom or making meaningful content for strangers . . . I come alive!

Consciously shifting from fear to love each day is the real miracle for me (shout-out to *A Course in Miracles* for introducing me to this concept). To this day, it still trips me out that I can pay my own bills without stressing, stealing, or begging my sister for money. Sometimes I have imposter syndrome, and my negative, fear-driven, dickhead brain becomes louder, like: *Who the hell do I think I am? I am a lazy drug-addict piece of shit. How could anyone love me? I should probably kill mys— STOP RIGHT THERE, LAURA. This isn't true. You know this isn't true.* And then, rather than living in that ghoulish, debilitating, morbid place for too long, I ask God to REMOVE my fear and REPLACE it with LOVE and unwavering faith that everything is going to work out better than I could have ever imagined. Then, I force myself to awkwardly power-walk through the hilly suburbs and say out loud: "I am so happy and grateful for the life I am living, that I have made it another day, and am a part of this miraculous universe. For my sobriety, and my children and husband and mother, and for food and shelter and friends and Anne and for my hardworking titties." Seriously, it's really difficult to be pissed off and grateful at the same time. Try it—I dare you.

CHAPTER 10

The Neurodivergent Bunch

My house is just a ten-minute power walk to a panoramic L.A. canyon. It's breathtaking—mostly because the air is so polluted, but it's also nice to look at. I walk up to that ravine pretty much daily because it helps me to feel slightly less loco, less batty, and less alarmed at the inevitable fact that I am 100 percent going to rest in eternal peace with the worms. It's my way of combating the immediate and mostly unwarranted panic I often wake up in. A random article I read online said that walking is the most effective way to rid yourself of anxiety because all anxiety is your body in fight-or-flight mode and walking releases that. I BELIEVE IT. So I wake up and tread through my trepidation, walk out my worry, hike away my hysteria, YOU GET IT. This morning walk (or as Tony Robbins coined it, 15 Minutes to Fulfillment) is my secret sauce for contentment. Except for that one day I almost got murdered . . .

There I was, glistening (not sweating!) and trudging up the radiant yet contaminated canyon, when I noticed a massive bird circling above my head. At first I thought it was a hawk, and then I thought it might be a vulture, and then I thought it was definitely a murderer. All of a sudden, six more giant, shaggy brown birds joined in the widening gyre, right above my spinning head. I thought *for sure* they were plotting to swoop down and peck me to death!

I went into full fight-or-flight mode (or as I call it, flight mode) and sprinted like mad back to the safety of the suburban streets. As I continued my walk back home, it hit me: I was acting out of fear. How unrealistic and self-involved it was to think that those vultures were out to get ME. Since when have you ever heard of a human being— even a bird-boned vegan—getting attacked by a gang of vultures?

The next day I mustered up the courage to go back up the canyon. I was sure the vultures would have had their fill of carrion and moved on, but there they were—*circling me again*! I was actually quite offended because they usually scavenge dead things—and I know I don't look great without makeup and a good night's sleep . . . but come on!

Instead of running away, I took a deep breath and chose in that moment to admire them and to be still in their presence. Suddenly the fear and anxiety left my body and a wave of complete calm washed through me. I watched in awe as these majestic dark birds with their beautifully broad wings flew so gracefully, so effortlessly, in their circular choreography, while barely flapping their wings. I yelled up to them, "Just FYI, these dark circles under my eyes are from lack of sleep but I'm very much still alive!"

My eyes started to well up at the beauty of them (and possibly some residual smoke from a wildfire nearby). But that morning I had made a conscious decision to be in love and awe instead of fear, and I swear the vultures and I were connected. I felt it and reminded myself the world doesn't have to be so scary. It can be beautiful. It's all how I choose to see it.

But this isn't a story about vultures. It's a story about choosing love over fear.

For the last few weeks, I have been deeply concerned for our son, Alfie. He is two years and two months old as I write this, and by the time you read it, I'll know more. I'll be less anxious then, but not today. Stephen took him to his two-year checkup while I was at home filming a brand deal for, of all things, a vibrator company. Stephen later told me that at the appointment, our very laid-back pediatrician asked questions like, "Is he waving?" No. "Is he clapping?" No. "Does he like to share?" That would be *no*. "Is he saying at least fifty words?" Ten words, tops, and five of those are animal noises.

Our usually relaxed doctor recommended that Alfie start speech therapy ASAP. "Early intervention is key," she said sternly. It was a phrase I would repeat many times over the next several months.

After he got home, Stephen looked worried. I was still filming the vibrator video, so I casually asked, "How'd it go?" He was so preoccupied that the bright pink sex toy in my hand didn't even faze him.

"Fine," he said, looking lost.

I didn't believe him. He gave Alfie some toy cars to play with, and then he finally told me what the doctor had said.

"She said Alfie needs speech therapy ASAP."

I nervously pushed the vibrator button on and off like a fidget toy.

"Then she handed me this rubbish." Stephen angrily handed me a pamphlet that read "Regional Center: Offering support for kids with developmental disabilities."

In shock, I stared at the pamphlet and then glanced over at Alfie, who was playing with his cars quietly.

"Why? Why did she hand you this?" I asked, confused.

"I don't fucking know. It's stupid. He's perfectly fine. I'm throwing this stupid thing away."

"Wait!" I said, pointing the vibrator at him sternly. "What did she say, EXACTLY?"

"She said he's speech delayed and that we should schedule an assessment at this regional center."

"For what? An assessment for what??"

"I don't know. She said something about insurance covering it if we get him assessed."

I pretended to be calm, even though my insides were in full panic. "Okay, yeah. I heard it's super common for little boys to have delayed speech. So cool, we'll get him assessed."

Underneath my false calm, my mom gut knew something more was going on and I started shaking. I still can't tell you if it was from nerves or because I had distractedly dialed up the vibrator to full speed.

"Can you turn that bloody thing off?"

"Yeah, sorry." We laughed nervously. Stephen tossed the pamphlet in the trash and we went on with our day. I finished filming, we played with the kids, made dinner, went through the bedtime routines. But inside, we were both obsessing about what the doctor had said and about the pamphlet.

That night I looked up developmental milestones for a two-year-old. Let's just say Alfie was not hitting many of them. Major speech delay, avoids eye contact, doesn't always respond to his name. He doesn't like to do imaginative play. (A broom is not a sword to him, it's a broom, and he fucking loves to sweep.) He didn't clap or point; he didn't wave. The more I researched, the more my heart sank: Autism. That's all I kept seeing, that word. Over and over.

Every time I would search something he did or didn't do, an article about autism came up. I realized very quickly that I knew nothing about it. I knew Elon Musk had it, *Rain Man*, and that's about all. I just didn't want Alfie to have to struggle in life; I didn't want him to have a hard time making friends. I just wanted him to be happy. I became obsessed with researching what was going on with our son. Sleepless night after sleepless night, reading countless studies and articles, watching videos, making checklists in my mind, worrying about his future.

The more I read, the more I saw how many signs Alfie had, the more convinced I became. He goes on his tippy-toes and he sometimes spins when he is excited. Was this stimming (self-stimulatory behavior, meaning repetitive or "unusual" movements or noises that help children manage their emotions)? Was it "normal"? I remember my nieces spinning and occasionally walking on their tippy-toes. Are they autistic? Is everyone autistic? What IS normal, anyway? He was also obsessed with toy cars and would turn them upside-down to spin their wheels, which was apparently another sign of autism, yet my best friend Maggie sent me a video of her son doing the same thing and he is not on the spectrum.

I've come to realize that autism doesn't mean something is "wrong" with you, it just means your brain is wired differently. But going through this as a parent is scary at first. Mainly because of how little I knew about it, and the negative, fear-driven articles I saw online. I remember when I would post videos or photos of Alfie, I would occasionally get well-meaning messages from other moms saying things like, "Alfie reminds me of my awesome son who has autism . . . Is your son on the spectrum?" Or, "My autistic daughter spins like that too and also ignores me when I call for her. Does Alfie have autism too?" At first the messages were sporadic, so I didn't think much of them. I dismissed them. But these moms weren't being mean, they were genuinely asking. Eventually, I brought the messages to Stephen.

"They don't know our son. They only see little snippets. ALL kids spin. ALL kids ignore their parents from time to time. All kids repeat random, seemingly nonsensical phrases around the house all day, don't clap or wave or point, and aggressively avoid eye contact with their parents . . . ," he said, his confidence appearing to dwindle.

Then the messages started coming more frequently. Two or three a week. At that point, it was hard to dismiss. I started to panic. I hate saying that now, *knowing* what I know now, but, at the time, I was very worried.

Stephen was angry at first when he saw all the comments, but I knew deep down that the well-meaning moms online were probably right. Alfie just checked off too many boxes. I had a feeling, and that intuition was confirmed even more when we went to a party at my friend Jill's house (the *South Park* aficionado). Anyway, that party turned out to be the biggest shit-show in town.

Leaving the house with a toddler and a newborn is hard enough, but when you've been isolated at home for a year because of a global pandemic that's changed the world as you know it, it's next-level irksome. The party at Jill's house was going to be our first social event in a year, and even though Maggie, Holly, and Jack—my closest friends since childhood—would be there, I did *not* want to go. To motivate myself, I decided to make a comedy sketch about the chaos of leaving the house with a newborn and a toddler. (It was literally the only way I could get myself to go—to film an improv comedy sketch around it—that's normal, right?) The video was actually pretty funny ("Did you pack the diapers?" "I don't know!" "Did you pack the dried mangos?" "I don't know!" "Where's our toddler?" "I don't know!!"), but the real-life aftermath of that day? Not so much.

I was also nervous about the party because Alfie sometimes struggles with things outside his normal routine. We thought it was because he was a pandemic baby and he hadn't socialized with other kids for his entire two years on this earth. So I was scared about how he would react. But Jill told me she got vegan pancakes especially for us, so we *had* to go. She also said, "You're fucking coming to my party." So we got in the car and went!

We walked into Jill's house and the party was all going smoothly . . . because there was no one in the house. Everyone was outside in the backyard, and as soon as Alfie stepped foot out the back and saw the people and kids and music and food and piñatas and lights and music . . . he started crying. Not little sniffles, but a full-blown meltdown. My best friend Jack came up and said "hi" to Alfie and I quickly snapped at him, "Jack, don't say hi to him!" My response startled even me. I guess I was trying to protect him. Alfie didn't have the ability to tell me if it was too loud or too bright, so instead he just screamed. Eventually he settled down and started playing with a toy car. All was good and well . . . for about thirty seconds, until Maggie's sweet two-year-old son approached Alfie and tried to take the toy car, as kids do, while saying, "NO!" Alfie. Lost. His. Shit. He just completely broke down. He was destroyed, and the meltdown doubled in intensity.

I was already so stressed by now, and it didn't help that my friends kept walking up to me with extremely concerned empathetic looks, asking, "*How ARE you, Laura?*" They had all just seen my Fourth Trimester video where I had a public mental breakdown, spilling intimate details about my postpartum depression. It was sweet of them to check in, but it also just made me cry even more. When Maggie and Jack told me, "Laura, I see you . . . we *see you*," with deep sympathy in their eyes, it was my turn to melt down.

When anyone asks me how I am in that *extremely* concerned way and I am NOT doing fine, it's my cue to blubber. I can't help it! You *know* what I'm talking about. I just came to eat some vegan pancakes and have a nice time, but instead Alfie and I were BOTH bawling our eyes out. Stephen looked so uncomfortable and tried his best to maintain small talk amid the chaos, but I could see the stress behind his eyes—and the spit-up on his shoulder—as he held Penelope and talked to Jason about real estate. We were in over our heads, drowning in a sea of balloons, party lights, spit-up, and tears.

I led Alfie back into the house so we could cry together alone. Maggie followed. I sat on the couch with Maggie, who was attempting to comfort me and tell me everything would be okay. In that moment, I wasn't so sure. We were trying to find the TV remote so we could put on a show to hopefully help Alfie calm down, but it was nowhere to be found. Alfie was now clawing at the window, trying to escape. Eventually we gave up on the search. Everything felt chaotic, uncertain, and a bit bleak. Maggie was so kind and generous, trying her best to tell me it would all be okay, but I had trouble believing her in that moment. I felt like such a failure as a mother. All of my friends seemingly had their children "under control" and were just casually enjoying the pancakes. Meanwhile my family couldn't keep our shit together—one member was wildly attempting to break through the window while my other child regurgitated tit milk all over Jill's outdoor sofa. It was hellish. Shortly after, Stephen and Poppy followed us inside. He handed Poppy to me and took Alfie outside for a walk to try to calm him.

Ten minutes later they came back . . . and Alfie was even more distraught. Then I saw a baby swing in the empty front yard, and in a desperate attempt to calm him down again, I put him in the swing. Unfortunately, it happened to be about three sizes too small for him. I tried to gently pull him out, but he wasn't budging. I'd gotten my own already distraught child stuck in a swing and Alfie was *really* losing it now. Stephen tried to get him out, then I tried again, then we tried together. Meanwhile, poor Maggie was holding her newborn baby AND mine. As we maneuvered Alfie and tried to free him, his meltdown just intensified, times ten. He was screaming, flailing, and wailing . . . His powerful front-kicks would have impressed Bruce Lee. Stephen was now on the verge of screaming and yelling right along with him. When we finally freed Alfie, I was beside myself. I told Maggie we were going to leave right then and there. I couldn't even go to the backyard to say goodbye to anyone. I was too distraught, too worried about Alfie, and too embarrassed that I couldn't stop crying. Also, too ashamed that I had perhaps failed as a mother altogether.

I hugged Maggie for a long time and she said that of course our friends would understand. But to me this didn't feel like a "normal" toddler meltdown, and my excuse that Alfie was a pandemic baby who wasn't used to social situations didn't feel quite true anymore. As Alfie and I continued bawling and Penelope upchucked titty milk on Stephen, Jack approached us.

"There you are, bitch!" he said.

"Jack, we're leaving. I love you, but I can't go back out there."

He paused, taking in the scene. "Wait, though—I want to get a group photo before you leave," he said breezily.

My eyes were now a deep, bloodshot red and Alfie was karate-chopping Jill's coffee table behind me. "Fuck off, Jack!" I said as kindly as I could. Jack completely understood and put his phone away. We said goodbye, got in the car, and drove home.

I was so worried about Alfie. I was scared by the intensity of his emotions at the party, and I had no clue what to do next. I just knew something wasn't right. I needed to figure out what was going on, and the prospect of that was overwhelming. What did that even look like? I lived for over thirty years with undiagnosed ADHD. I failed classes, constantly got in trouble, and I assumed it was all because I was an idiot—hence my book titles. I knew that whatever happened, we had to get Alfie help as soon as possible. I didn't want Alfie to spend his life feeling like something was "wrong" with him, as I had done.

I know every child is different. Some toddlers have easily distracted, work-obsessed parents who love them, and these children are early talkers and hit all the milestones. But Alfie needed more structure and more undivided attention. He needed MORE from us. I am just SO incredibly grateful that we woke up when we did. We made a pact to work less, be on our phones less, and make a much bigger effort to help him learn and grow. Once we'd decided to help Alfie instead of staying in denial, we asked our pediatrician for another Regional Center pamphlet because Stephen had trashed the first one.

From what I had been reading, it looked like Alfie had echolalia, where he repeats the same phrases over and over throughout the day. He would just randomly yell "MONKEY DOGGIE!" multiple times a day even if there was no monkey or doggie in sight. It's adorable, and I honestly hope he never stops even when he's twenty-three. Apparently, Einstein also had echolalia. Oh, and if one more person tells me that "Einstein didn't speak until he was four," I'm going to lose it, although, to be honest, it *is* kind of reassuring. Keep telling me. The more I read, the more my confusion grew. Disability? Disorder? Difference? Condition? Was autism something to be feared, or celebrated, or both?

We were still at that point of being not entirely sure what was going on—whether Alfie was just speech-delayed or had sensory issues or was autistic. And then . . . it became undeniable.

Alfie started regressing. The words he once knew were gone, or on the back burner for reasons I will never fully understand. He just one day stopped saying "Mama," "Dada," "milk," and "shoes." He used to call shoes "sha-bahs." Every time we put them on, it sounded like we were celebrating a Jewish holiday and we loved it. And then he just stopped. He stopped looking at us. Stopped calling our names. Stopped responding to *his* name. We were suddenly struggling to connect with the boy we once knew. At night, Stephen and I held each other and cried because we just didn't know what was happening with our boy. We didn't know when the unexplainable regression would stop, or how we could help him. What concerned me the most was when he stopped smiling. He actually looked scared at times, like he didn't know what was happening either. And so, any doubts I'd had about whether Alfie was autistic or not went out the window. This regression confirmed it for me.

I knew we needed to stop worrying and start helping him immediately.

Once Stephen, too, believed our son was autistic, a fire lit within him. He put on his fierce, unrelenting advocate hat and became rightfully obsessive about getting Alfie the support he needed. Early intervention is key, they say, yet it took an incredible amount of perseverance to get Alfie assessed. Eventually we started going on what would be a never-ending string of appointments. After the Regional Center asked us eight million questions about Alfie's capabilities, Stephen and I looked at each other and nearly cried. Without saying a word, we both realized that perhaps we hadn't been doing enough. This wasn't a pity party or guilt trip. This was us taking a good, hard look at ourselves and our parenting thus far and saying, "Where could we have done better? How can we DO better?" We got really honest with each other at that moment. We talked about how we had been physically there pretty much all the time, but sometimes we became distracted by work and social media and stupid shit that just does not matter in comparison. We hadn't been fully present with Alfie. We would play with him for a bit and then scroll on our phones. We would just give him everything and anything he wanted rather than encouraging him to use his voice. Perhaps we were the problem. Perhaps we'd failed him. Perhaps our need to be successful had been more of a priority than teaching our son basic language. Now, I know that we are not the reason he has a speech delay or sensory issues, but Alfie's regression woke us up in a profound way. It made us realize that we were perhaps prioritizing the wrong things. Nothing (other than our sobriety) was as important as being fully present with each other and our kids. Work could wait, videos could wait, music could wait. Our child needed us fully present . . . right here and now.

At that moment, we both hit a sort of rock bottom. We made the decision that we would go to any lengths to help Alfie succeed in this world. And by "succeed" I DO NOT mean "fit in," I do not mean "get famous or rich," and I do not mean become "neurotypical." By "succeed" I mean be happy, fulfilled, safe, and at peace with himself and the world. We love him so very much, but we'd brushed off the fact that he wasn't hitting his milestones. We just thought,

"He's perfect! He will get to the milestones in his own time!" We just thought he was developing at his own pace, which he was, but we didn't realize he desperately needed so much more. Overnight I became a BETTER mother. I committed fully to teaching this kid how to speak, and how to be happy and safe. I knew this was going to become a near full-time job, and I was committed and ready to take it on.

The actual assessment with the Regional Center went as badly as it possibly could have. It was over Zoom, so how could it not? Poppy was on my breast, Alfie was screaming, and the dog shat on the floor—the shit-show was literal. The assessment went on for what seemed like hours. Alfie was particularly defiant that day and wouldn't do any of the tasks the woman asked him to do. We knew he was capable of doing a lot of them—solving puzzles, identifying animals, showing us where his different body parts were—but he completely refused to do any of it. Exhausted and exasperated, I asked the woman point-blank, "Do you think he has autism?"

Wanna know what she said? She said she thought *he was just spoiled* and needed more discipline. I am not kidding! She also told us that he was developmentally a year behind where he needed to be. We were shattered, but deep down I knew she was wrong.

During this time, I had been avoiding my sister's calls for days. I wasn't ready to talk to her about Alfie. My mom had been in deep denial about Alfie possibly having autism, constantly assuring us there was "nothing wrong with him" and "he is perfect." I call that having her "grandma glasses on." And in her defense, those things are true: there is nothing inherently "wrong" with him and he is "perfect," and he also happens to be autistic. It was tough for me to talk about it to anyone, to be honest. I didn't know how they'd react and didn't know if I wanted to subject myself to anyone's reaction or advice. Finally, after ignoring her calls for nearly a week, I picked up when Colleen called. I left Stephen with the kids and I walked up the foggy hill so I could be alone and have some space. I told her about Alfie and how I was pretty convinced he was autistic. Colleen paused and then compassionately said, "He is so lucky to have you two as his parents and I am so excited for you and this journey."

She assured me that Alfie was going to thrive. She then asked, "Do you think Stephen is on the spectrum?"

I paused.

YES . . . YES, I do . . .

In fact, what we had recently discovered is that Stephen acted as a child exactly the same way that Alfie acts. I'm talking very specific traits. Stephen didn't want to share toys or play with the other kids. He had obsessive interests with cars and would turn them over to spin their wheels. He would stim by biting the noses off all his stuffed animals—a very specific quirk—and ALFIE DOES THE SAME EXACT THING. His favorite owl's nose is bitten off and my mom had to go to four different shops to find a replacement owl to send to us.

Many kids on the spectrum have little sense of danger and will sprint into the street with no warning. Moobs (Stephen's nickname for his mother) used to put a leash on Stephen because he would dart off. It might sound horrible to leash your kid, but she was just trying to keep him safe. Which brings me to Stephen's next autistic trait . . . MAKING UP WORDS. Stephen literally calls his mother MOOBS and his father DINGLE. When Stephen and I did a checklist for adults with autism spectrum disorder, "making up words" was on the list, and Stephen is the only adult I know who does it all day, every day.

As I walked to the canyon, my sister and I continued to talk about how Stephen might also be on the spectrum. It started making more sense why Alfie was the way he was. I finally reached the canyon, still talking to Colleen. I looked around at the soaring vultures and the scenic hills before turning to make my way back down toward the house. And then I saw her. My guiding light.

"Oh, there's Anne!" I said excitedly.

"Who's Anne?" Colleen asked.

"She's my ninety-eight-year-old earth angel, also known as my neighbor. She walks up steep hills every day all by herself, and every single time I bump into her I ask her important questions. I've already asked her if she believes in God, what's the most important lesson she'd give to young people, and whether she thinks Kegels are worth it!"

I started hurrying toward Anne. She had her gray braids tied with yellow bands, and her silver cane gleamed as if it were magic.

"I think I'll ask her what the purpose of life is!" I said as I put Colleen on speaker.

"Hi, Laura," Anne said. By now, she was used to me accosting her on her strolls.

"Hi!" I panted. "Quick question! I won't keep you long! But . . . what's the purpose of life?"

I could feel Colleen's mortification through the phone. Colleen struggles to order a delivery pizza, let alone approach a stranger and ask them deeply personal questions. Anne got pensive.

"To live," she said. "I believe every single person has so much potential within them and the saddest thing in the world to me is when they do not reach their personal potential, whatever that may be."

I swear Anne tells me exactly what I need to hear each time I see her. I immediately took this to mean that I needed to do whatever I could for Alfie and Penelope, to help them reach their personal potential and thrive. It was clear to me that Alfie needed more support than what we were giving him. I was prepared to go to any lengths to help him reach his personal potential. I said goodbye to Anne and then to Colleen, and I hurried home.

At two years and three months old, Alfie was diagnosed with autism Level 3. There are only three levels. This came as a huge shock to us. When we went in for the official non-Zoom assessment he was playful, he made eye contact, he asked for "more bananas." But the woman assessing him said he was inattentive, nonverbal, and that he needed the greatest amount of therapy possible. The official diagnosis itself wasn't shocking, because deep down I knew he was autistic. It's classified as a "developmental disorder," but "disorder" sounds *entirely* negative and I don't believe that autism is. At all. Sure, he may have challenges outside the norm, but most of his quirks I don't see as negative. He looks at the world in a wonderfully unique way, and we need that.

Level 3 is labeled as "severely autistic," but I don't like that term at all. "Severe" is "bad" or "undesirable," and that's not AT ALL what Alfie is to me. If anything, he's intensely creative, curious, and affectionate. He has a hunger to learn and connect and explore. He sees the world in a different way than most, and what a GIFT that is. NOTHING about him is BAD or UNDESIRABLE. Well, I suppose I could live without the high-pitched screams and flailing limbs . . . But it seems to me that he sees the world in such an intense way that maybe it becomes overwhelming at times, and so I ask: "How can I help you, dear Alfie?"

If you look up autism spectrum disorder, the CDC says it's a developmental disability that can cause significant social, communication, and behavioral challenges. Hmm . . . Okay. But why did they leave out that autism can also lead to an incredible ability to think logically, to memorize and learn information quickly? Why did they fail to mention that it can cause exceptional honesty and reliability? Alternate problem-solving and an incredible sense of wonderment about the world? Why isn't any of that included?

It's like if someone tells me to describe my husband and I say, "Oh, he doesn't have many friends, he can't cook, and one time nine years ago he had cybersex and blamed it on a hacker." What a dick I'd be! What I should really say is that he's the funniest man I know, an incredible musician, and a dedicated father. Sure, he struggles, but his challenges and perseverance are part of who he is. He is just as he should be and so is my son. Oh, and I should probably mention, at forty-seven years old Stephen was just officially diagnosed with autism.

It takes all kinds of brains to make a world go 'round, so I believe personality differences in autism can also be great gifts, not *just* deficits. Many autistic people don't love eye contact all the time, and SO WHAT? Who is that harming? What is the obsession with STARING into each other's eyes ALL THE TIME? As for stimming? Everyone stims in their own way, but autistic people just tend to do it more noticeably. I think Alfie's spinning and hand flapping are absolutely adorable and I don't see anything wrong with it. So long as nothing's self-injurious, I don't see the problem. Some autistic people don't love socializing and prefer to be alone. Temple Grandin, a well-known autistic woman, has famously said, "What would happen if the autism gene was eliminated from the gene pool? You would have a bunch of people standing around in a cave, chatting and socializing and not getting anything done." Hilarious.

I'm not trying to downplay the struggles that come with autism, but I choose to focus on the good things about it and encourage Alfie's unique strengths while helping him with his struggles. We are a whole family of neurodivergents. Stephen and I were both diagnosed with ADHD, Stephen and Alfie are both on the spectrum, and Poppy? Well, only time will tell. Perhaps she will be the only neurotypical in the family, who knows? Who cares? Our differences are what make the world go 'round.

Neurodiverse people experience the world in unique ways, and I think this should be celebrated. There is an unfortunate stigma for the one in five people whose brains happen to learn and think differently—autism, dyslexia, apraxia, ADHD, OCD, and more. Why not learn how best to accommodate these beautiful brains rather than continue with the prejudiced, ableist mindsets that are so prevalent today? The fact is these perceived deficits, disorders, and disabilities also come with incredible strengths that have helped better our world in previously unimaginable ways.

After just one month of getting the proper speech and child development therapy for Alfie, he regained his lost words and learned *many* more. He's expressing his wants and needs beautifully and it's the coolest thing to see. We also cut gluten out of his diet to see if he perhaps had a gut issue that was causing brain fog for him. I know this sounds quacky . . . but dude: It seemed to work for him. To be clear, I in NO WAY say "diet will cure autism." Nor do I believe that autism can or should be "cured"—that's not the goal for us. But once Alfie had the regression, we were desperate to get him back and willing to try anything. We had been advised and read that cutting out gluten and dairy could help with brain fog and gut health. I have to say, for him it seemed to make a difference. Within a week of changing his diet, he was voluntarily making more eye contact and wanted to connect with us. His meltdowns were much less frequent, he seemed happier and more playful, and he was regaining words. I can't say for certain what caused the change or whether it was a combination of things.

I also had been much more present with him, giving him my undivided attention, slowing down my language for him, repeating words, and narrating literally everything we were doing, to help his speech. "Up up UP!" as we walked up the stairs. Now, every time Alfie takes our hands to bring us somewhere (it's called "hand leading" in the literature and I thought every kid did this), we repeat our names. This was one of the tools we used during his regression when he stopped saying "Mama" and "Dada." I remember I hadn't heard him say those words in WEEKS and it was devastating. I wondered if I would ever hear them again. So every time he led us and his hand would touch mine, I'd say, "Mama, Mama, Mama," and then I'd go where he wanted me to go. After a couple of days of this, he approached me and took my hand to lead me somewhere, most likely the kitchen for more almond butter, and I pulled back. He looked at me like I had lost my mind. "Why aren't you coming with me?" his big doe eyes said back at me. He continued to pull on my hand. I pulled back, waiting. He became a little frustrated. And then he looked at me, right in my eyes, and said, "Mama." I cried, Stephen cried. I shot up and said, "Yes, my sweetie?! Where would you like to go?! What would you like to do?! Thank you for saying my name!"

"Dada" came about four days after. We cried again that day, and every little milestone is SO meaningful. Every little bit of progress he makes is so big and special. "Repeat and expand" has been incredibly helpful for me with his language. Once he mastered "Mama," every time he took my hand, we added, "Mama go . . ." Now, as I write this, Alfie is two years and five months old, and he says, "Mama go with me!" He is making so much progress every day and I feel closer to him than ever before. I am now truly present with him, and I've learned so much from the therapists and from the other parents who have reached out to us. This unexpected journey has been, yes, sometimes a struggle—but also an absolute gift.

I'm just so glad we didn't stick our heads in the sand and ignore the delays. Believe me, it was tempting. I've decided that I will accept nothing less than for Alfred to live a wonderful life. We will do anything and everything we can to teach him and, more importantly, to understand HIS world. We will make sure he gets the extra support he needs to learn necessary skills to help him function and thrive more easily in the world. I only care that he is happy and safe, reaches his personal potential, and feels fully accepted for who he is. That he has the tools and the support to get where he wants to go. I know I have so much more to learn and that we have a long road ahead . . . full of challenges, blissful moments, and everything in-between. I firmly believe with all my heart that the universe does not give us more than we can handle. Alfie and Penelope were meant for us and they are exactly as they should be.

One day when we were at Alfie's therapy appointment, he was lying on the floor, playing with a toy car and looking completely content. He was a little boy examining his toy car exactly like Stephen used to do as a kid. The therapist started asking him to sit up and play with the car while sitting up. Maybe because that's what "typical" kids do? Is there a "right" way to play with toy cars? I've never seen medical journals come out with articles about the dangers of rolling a Hot Wheels around while lying safely on the ground, have you? He looked peaceful and perfectly content in the moment. This woman was bent on "correcting" him, but I didn't agree. It seemed harmless, like he just wanted to experience the car from a different perspective.

I thought about all the times my own mom told me that I was perfect just the way I was, despite being "different"—despite me struggling in school and what the world perceived as my "faults." How she just let me be the sometimes overly social class clown because it's what came naturally to me. It made me happy, even though the teachers often corrected me for it (which is also understandable). But my mother encouraged me to be exactly me, and here I am making millions of people laugh for a living. That pure, unconditional love is what I felt for Alfie—the same absolute acceptance my mom had given me.

When we were back at home, Alfie was lying peacefully on the ground, admiring his toy cars from a different perspective. I could have told him to sit up, but he looked perfectly happy there on the ground. So instead, I lay down across from him on the floor and played with the cars that way too. Our eyes met as we drove the tiny cars down the blue rug and the look in his eyes said so very clearly, *"See, Mom? Isn't it cool from this perspective?"*

And yes. Yes it was.

I have to constantly keep making the decision to live in LOVE as my mind often runs to fear, and it's always progress and never perfection. I make the choice to focus on and nurture our strengths rather than worry about our so-called weaknesses, because it feels better. I'm even grateful that I am a recovering alcoholic! We're so bombarded with grim facts regarding addiction that it seems impossible to look at the bright side, but YOU BETTER BELIEVE I HAVE FOUND IT! For one thing, recovering addicts are natural risk-takers and so long as we are sober, that can be a great benefit to society. We often take on careers that others may find too terrifying or stressful to consider. One woman I met in AA said to me casually, "Yeah, I work in a psych ward for suicidal children. I love it." She thrives under high stress, and our world benefits from that.

It's back to making that decision to focus on what we DO want rather than what we DON'T. Our assets, rather than our deficits. I even consider my ADHD, as frustrating as it may be, a blessing! It's probably why I am so spontaneous and creative. My impulsivity and ability to think outside the box have been real assets in my work. Sure, I wait until the last possible minute to get it done . . . BUT IT GETS DONE, DAMMIT! Stephen spent his whole life trying to understand why he was different before he was confirmed autistic. He never received any support, therapy, or help with his social and communication struggles. Luckily, he also had parents who nurtured his special interests, which were—you guessed it— synthesizers. He was so obsessed with them that he wouldn't even make it into the classroom. His mom dropped him off at school, and he went in the front door and out the back to sneak home and write music all day while she was working. He got a record deal at fifteen years old, and today he is one of the world's biggest film composers. Sure, he struggles to connect with others and keep things in order, but he thrives in other areas and we choose to focus on those. Alfie and Penelope will be no different. We will focus on what they love and are naturally drawn to. We'll nurture their strengths while providing them with the support they need for their challenges.

I personally think neurodiversity is crucial for the human race. Maybe we just need to practice more love, tolerance, and acceptance for those who are different. One therapist said that we needed to teach Alfie not to spin in the grocery store. I told her that so long as he is not in the knife aisle, not only do I not mind if he spins in the store but I would be joining him.

And to my lovely neurotypical readers who maybe didn't know much about autism or neurodivergence before this, I ask that next time you're at the grocery store and you see a kid melting down to the ground, spinning, or making loud noises like you may have never heard, please don't be too quick to judge. Perhaps you're not looking at a "spoiled" or "out of control" kid with "bad parents," but rather a child who experiences the world differently than you do. Perhaps they're doing the best they can in this loud, bright, busy, sensory-overloaded world. What if the grocery stores ARE too bright, and the car horns ARE too loud, and perhaps we as a society could stand to calm the fuck down a bit?

When things are getting tough or scary, I often think to myself: *What would Anne do?* A few days before writing this, I was once again blessed to cross paths with the one and only, my guiding light, my enlightened matriarch, Anne. I asked her how she was doing. She paused, catching her breath, then told me she was feeling weaker than she ever had before. She was tired and said her balance was starting to fail her. Then she smiled knowingly and said with steadfast assurance that it was her dream to drop dead while walking up this very hill. She told me she didn't think she had much time left and could think of no better way to go than while trudging up this steep, smoggy hillside. I teared up and then so did she (maybe from the smog, we don't know).

I marveled that even though she felt she was fading, Anne continued to boldly climb up that steep hill. She wasn't wasting her precious time on this wondrous earth by dwelling on what was seemingly wrong, but instead she continued to *move forward*. She didn't fear the uneven gravel beneath her feet or the circling vultures above her head as she marched on and reveled in the beauty of the now.

She placed her delicate, shaking hand over mine and looked straight into my weepy eyes:

"Honey, you're not dead yet. Keep going. Keep going. KEEP. GOING."

Acknowledgments

I have to start by thanking my incredible husband, Stephen. You've encouraged me to be fearless and bold and write my truth since the very beginning. You reassured me that it was okay to write about even our darkest times because rigorous honesty and courage are more important to you than appearing "perfect." This is what I love about you. Well, one of the many things. I also love when you attempt to twerk. That never gets old. I love you more today, ya know?

To my incredible son, Alfie. You continue to amaze me every day. You are so very funny, intelligent, unique, and creative. Please know that you are always loved and accepted for exactly who you are. Know this. You inspire me every day and I would be honored to spin with you until the end of time.

My cheeky, stunning daughter, Penelope. You're eight months as I write this and just started to crawl. You are going places! Literally. I love everything about you dear Poppy. How you thrive on connection and cuddles. Your smile and those eyes really do solve ALL world problems every time. You inspire me daily and fill my heart with so much joy it makes me physically sick. I love you sweet baby.

Thank you to both my children for letting me tell our story. I will be sure to pay for as much therapy as you both shall need. Try your best to not give a flying fuck what anyone else thinks. Just be yourselves, lean on each other, fill your days with love, and don't ever die. I love you both until the end of time.

Thank you to my mother, Marilyn, for your endless support and unconditional love. I know having an internet-famous daughter who shares every intimate detail of her life can't always be easy. So thank you, Mama, for emboldening me to tell my story, even when it's uncomfortable. You have sacrificed so much for your daughters and I AM the luckiest girl in the entire world because of you. I love you forever.

To my sisters, Colleen and Tracy, for putting up with my shit. For protecting me. For helping to keep me alive. Thank you for your love and tolerance and grace. You've both taught me so much. I wish we lived closer.

My daddy. Thank you for showing me that it is okay to be different. To question authority and think outside the box. Also thank you for passing on your tall lanky genetics, they have served me well in my comedy career.

Moobs and Dingle. When I tell you I LUCKED OUT in the in-law department! Thank you for always being there when I call. Thank you for letting us share such personal information about our lives with the public. You have both been so kind, compassionate, and understanding through it all. I see why Stephen is the spectacular man he is today. It's because of you two. I love you both, so very much.

ACKNOWLEDGMENTS

My sweet as pie, super-human nanny, Carla. Without you, this book would never have gotten done. I love you so much and so do both my children. Thank you for treating them with such kindness and respect. I am so grateful to you. Truly, you're a fucking lifesaver.

My LA besties, Maggie, Jack, Holly, and Jill. Ya'll are my rocks and I'm sorry I don't always text back. Thank you for letting me include you in my book. Thank you for always being there for me since CHILDHOOD. Thank you for the inevitable belly laughs, for not giving a shit that I am famous, and for always making it a safe space. (If any of you decide to move out of Los Angeles I will murder you.)

To Dina, for helping me write this book. For the countless hours we sat on the phone as I broke down to you, scatterbrained and sleep-deprived. You never judged me, not once. You were so patient and kind with me always. You cared about making this book great just as much as I did. You even continued to help me through a devastating personal tragedy. I can't express how much that meant to me. You are simply incredible, Dina, and I am forever grateful to you.

My amazing editor, Jeremie. Thank you for the countless hours you put into this book. I can tell that you really care. Your talent is astounding and you're the perfect amount of blunt without being an asshole. Thank you, Jeremie. To many more.

Larry! My manager. You've been with me from the beginning. Hyping me up when I need it most. Thank you for your innovative brain. Your patience, creativity, and unrelenting drive. I'm very lucky to have you by my side.

My lawyer, MATT! You represented me when I was broke, green, and cray-cray! But you saw something in me and helped me when no one else would. I'll never forget it. You're the NICEST, most HONEST lawyer in all of L.A., and that is a fact.

Molly, for your kindness, patience, and professionalism. Thank you for making this process easy(ish) and fun!

Elisa! Thanks for helping me not get sued. Your energy makes me feel safe and I really love your accent.

Last, but certainly not least, to Oliver, my one-eyed pug. You never stopped putting up a fight, until the very end. You were the sweetest, most hilarious dog I ever did know. Thank you for being so kind and gentle to our son in your last days. You are why he fell in love with dogs. May you rest in peace, sweet boy.